Lamplighters

Exploring
Spirituality
in New Contexts

Edited by
Bernadette Flanagan PBVM
and David Kelly OSA

VERITAS

First published 2004 by
Veritas Publications
7/8 Lower Abbey Street
Dublin 1
Ireland
Email publications@veritas.ie
Website www.veritas.ie

ISBN 1 85390 762 6

Cover image by Stephen Killick
Printed in the Republic of Ireland by Betaprint Dublin

*Veritas books are printed on paper made from the wood pulp of managed
forests. For every tree felled, at least one tree is planted, thereby renewing
natural resources.*

Contents

Contributors

Pauline Campbell is a member of the Religious Sisters of Charity. Her chapter is a response to her experience as an outreach worker with SPIRASI (Spiritan Asylum Services Inititiative) where she worked with survivors of torture.

David Coghlan SJ is a faculty member of the School of Business Studies, Trinity College, Dublin where he teaches action research. One of his recent publications (with Teresa Brannick) is *Doing Action Research in Your Own Organization* (London: Sage, 2001).

Jack Finnegan SDB is Associate Professor of Spirituality at Milltown Institute, Dublin. He is a founding member and chairperson of the All Ireland Spiritual Guidance Association (AISGA).

Bríd Fitzgerald is married with two children and is employed by Balally Parish, Dublin, as Coordinator of Pastoral Services. She has been involved with the Faith and Light community for the past eighteen years, is a founding member of the Ballinteer community and is currently serving as Vice-National Coordinator of Faith and Light in Ireland.

Bernadette Flanagan PBVM is Head of the School of Spirituality and Postgraduate Theology at Milltown Institute. Her previous book was *The Spirit of the City: Voices from Dublin's Liberties* (Dublin: Veritas, 1999)

Thomas G. Grenham SPS has worked as a missionary priest in Kenya and has been involved in developing pastoral and religious education programmes for culturally diverse communities of faith while working as adjunct faculty member at Boston College.

Joe Killick, who has been involved in theatre as a director, lighting designer, scriptwriter and lecturer for more than thirty years, graduated in 2003 with an MA in Applied Spirituality from Milltown Institute, and also holds a teaching licentiate in speech and drama from the Leinster School of Music.

Brian O'Leary SJ is Associate Professor of Spirituality at Milltown Institute. He has published widely on spirituality topics in *The Way, Review for Religious, Manresa* and *Cahiers de Spiritualité Ignatienne*.

Michael O'Sullivan SJ has worked as a missionary priest in Chile. He is a lecturer in the Department of Spirituality at Milltown Institute and is currently completing a doctorate on the challenge of male violence against women on the doctrine of salvation.

Seán McKiernan spent his childhood on a farm and this has given him a sense of wonder and awe at the absolute power, harmony and beauty of nature and creation. He views creation as a privileged source of God's unique revelation.

Noreen Murray, a member of the congregation of the Daughters of Mary and Joseph, is a former nurse. Her article arises from a lifelong search for seeds of Resurrection in the midst of the suffering of mental illness, and the desire to see practical, integrative outcomes in the fields of spirituality and psychiatry.

Eileen Pugh has been married for twenty-one years and has four daughters. She has been accompanying individuals and groups on their spiritual journey for the past fourteen years. She gives talks to secondary school groups and, with her husband, to engaged couples on the Mount Argus pre-marriage course. Eileen is currently Co-ordinator of the Adult Education Diploma in Spiritual Enrichment at Milltown Institute.

Denis Robinson CSSp has worked as a missionary priest in Ghana and as a staff member of the Institute of Formative Spirituality in Duquesne University, Pittsburgh. He is currently Director of Postgraduate Programmes in Spirituality (Taught) at Milltown Institute.

Nuala Rothery has retired as a counselling psychologist and trainer and is now spending her time travelling and cultivating her garden and her friends.

Preface

Most of us remember how we marked the arrival of the new millennium. As the dating of the calendar year underwent that infrequent event of total digital changeover we wondered what challenges such a moment might pose. Would our computers fall victim to the millennium bug, would aeroplanes fall from the sky at midnight, how long would it take to adjust to using a new date formula in correspondence?

In a less obviously dramatic way the forms and expressions of spirituality in Ireland are also undergoing significant change at this time. The prayer styles seen in the churches of the new ethnic groups, especially those of African origin, have not previously been part of the Irish spiritual landscape. The demand for personal spiritual guidance and prayer accompaniment has led to the development of a professional network and in-service education structure for those in these ministries through the All Ireland Spiritual Guidance Association (AISGA). The visit of the relics of Thérèse of Lisieux and the launch of the film *The Passion of the Christ* both drew enormous public interest.

In the context of these unfolding changes, Milltown Institute decided in 2000 to focus the expertise of the staff of the Department of Spirituality on responding to these new challenges. The primary aim was to assist those who facilitate the spiritual journey in this new landscape in developing the maps required for their ministry. The essays that follow arise from the questions of 'applied spirituality'. The earlier essays in the collection engage some of the emerging issues theoretically;

the later essays aim to provide hints of the sense and texture of the new spiritual challenges. My hope is that the authors of these theoretical and practical works may act as lamplighters, enabling us to discern the diverse traces of the Spirit at work in new ways today.

Bernadette Flanagan
Pentecost 2004

PART ONE

Current Issues
in Applied Spirituality

The Nature and Meaning of Applied Spirituality

DR DENIS ROBINSON CSSp

The Beginning and the End

All spirituality has its roots in the lived experience of God. For this reason Christian spirituality is primarily concerned with the awareness of and response to the invitation to enter into a personal and communal relationship with the Triune God who is experienced as actively and intimately present within us and all creation. The development of the art and discipline of spirituality reflects this fundamental reality and has, over the centuries, helped Christians understand and grow in this dynamic and creative faith relationship. The goal of Christian spirituality, therefore, is to help people understand how and why they are drawn to the Transcendent; to discover the most authentic and appropriate means of living this relationship, and to live and share this experience of the sacred in relationship with others.

As a believing community we know that God's self-revelation in love can touch us to the core of our being and reveal that we truly are created in the image and likeness of God. In this relationship we discover a purpose and self-identity that is more profound and transcendent than seems possible. As we try to express what God means to us while our lives unfold and circumstances allow, we come to realise that we live as the recipients of a committed, covenanted love, which invites us to the fullness of life. The ultimate motive for spiritual growth is the desire to remember and experience anew God's love and active presence, and participate fully in this love.

This relationship is the source of extraordinary knowledge and experience. It has the power to integrate all aspects of our personality into a coherent whole, in spite of our all too evident fragmentation and inadequacies. It creates an interior reality that can encompass the God of the universe and, at the same time, propel into the world a people astonished by – and wanting to share – the experience of a profound love. It draws us inward, into the secret recesses of the soul and reveals a world of meaning that is enthralling and captivating. It is a relationship so significant that it not only makes possible a more integrated life, but also provides us with meaning, insight, and ultimate purpose. It is no wonder that being in this relationship is transforming, in that it has the capacity to continually bring us to the point of apparent human fulfilment only to reveal a deeper awareness of the transcendent possibilities within us, or bring us to the point of despair only to reveal a more profound truth.[1]

To be consciously aware of and participate in this very real relationship with God does not violate any aspect of our personhood or individuality; it is not an imposition. There is a dynamic relational and interactive process at work, with a language and logic all its own.[2] It exceeds the boundaries of all other relationships and yet includes and promotes them all. It always involves change, purification, and maturation. It makes us want to alter our behaviour and modify our thinking. For all these reasons, and more, we know that the essence of Christian spirituality is the intimacy of the human spirit in dialogue with the Divine Spirit. It is an intimacy that generates life and makes possible the 'fullness of human flourishing, the redemption of the whole world.'[3] The beginning and end of spirituality is this dynamic relation between God and ourselves.

Making Connections

What is the connection between Spirituality and Applied Spirituality? While there is no doubt that we have received a most singular and gratuitous gift in being created in the image and likeness of God, this fundamental connectedness between God's life and our life is not always immediately obvious. Only gradually do we come to understand the presence, activity and relevance of God, in Himself and in our lives. For the vast majority of people the realisation that God's being and our being are inextricably bound together has to be discovered. How then do we come to experience and know God as personal and loving, as one pre-eminently involved in every aspect of life? This is where the concept of spirituality meets the lived reality of spirituality, where theory and praxis meet.

Spirituality reflects a dynamic way of being in relationship, it reflects the need for people to appropriate and interpret the activity of God in themselves and their world if relationship with God is to be real and meaningful. Applied spirituality is founded on the premise that we meet and come to know God in everyday existence. This orientation cultivates a willingness to accept the challenge of looking for God in the people, events and things of ordinary life. It calls for us to become critically reflective, to dialogue with all aspects of life and world in the search for God.

As Rahner has pointed out, creation and human life is the context of God's self-revelation.[4] It is also the context of our response. We are not spirits capable of unimpeded union with God. Ours is always a gradual discovery of God and a gradual discovery of self in God. Since we can unintentionally live out our lives without really knowing who we are, applied spirituality invites us to search for our true selves in relationship with the Transcendent by developing a conscious sensitivity to the presence and working of God in self, in others, and in all the circumstances of life. With this perspective our inner restlessness, the disquiet we experience, the questions and doubts that assail us, the trials and tribulations, the wonder, joys and pleasures of life are experienced as vestiges of the Divine, as means to encounter the sacred and discover the personal meaning and relevance of God. In becoming so aware and critically reflective we accept the challenge to develop a real, involved spirituality; we assume responsibility for our own relationship with God. The Christian tradition, through its dogma and practices, reflects the truth of the experience of God distilled through the ages. This, in turn, creates an understanding of and expectation about God, but it is only when we have caught a glimpse of God within that we develop a genuine appreciation of this wisdom and truth and a fundamental trust in the meaningfulness of existence. An authentic encounter with God can only grow out of the dialogue between faith and experience, because this is when God's reality becomes more urgent, more convincing.

A Glimpse of the God Within[5]
The foundation of the contemporary understanding of spirituality is based on the realisation of the role and significance of personal experience inasmuch as 'the world of experience is the basic source of

all understanding.'[6] Experience has to be an integral part of our relationship with God since it is only through the world of human experience that we have access to the reality that is God. How could we know of God's self-revelation except through human experience? The fact is that 'we do not come into the world with a ready-made self. Rather we enter life with a capacity to become, which is shaped by our experiences of reality.'[7] The self is formed and reformed, and even deformed, through interaction with reality. In the labour of contingency, challenge and change, in those moments that disturb or delight us, our attention is drawn beyond ourselves in search of ultimate reasons and answers. At such moments we engage life and meaning at its most fundamental level. These instances of ambiguity and doubt confront us with the naked truth of total dependence on God. We are not the source of our own being or happiness. We know and feel the transience of life and the limitations of our personal existence; we know the madness, the injustices and uncertainty of life. These are experiences that generate critical reflection, they challenge us, evoke some response, demand our consideration, and they are the catalysts to an encounter with the Divine.

As St Augustine suggested long ago, the restless tensions, those nagging questions, and the moments of wonder and joy transport us beyond self-preoccupation into the realm of the Divine. It is in these experiences that we meet God. When we are taken out of our routines and beyond the security of certainty and predictability, our experiences have the potential to reveal the Divine. This has been the basis of the Christian tradition from the very beginning. Critical experiences are moments of transition that propel us out of the ordinary and into the transcendent. In and through human experience we discover the presence, reality and activity of God. We believe in God because in some way or other we have experienced Him. Life itself is the basis for our experience of God, and faith is our response to this experience. This is the way it was from the beginning and will continue until the end of time.

Pope John Paul II speaks of the disclosure of God in and through human experience when he says:

> God is co-experienced and co-known, co-present and co-active, in the interruptions of human experience, in the drive towards self-transcendence, in the dynamic intentionality of the subject, in the sting of contingency, in the quest for meaning, in 'the search for

truth', in the insatiable need for good, hunger for freedom, nostalgia for the beautiful and the voice of conscience.[8]

Experience is the foundation of our knowledge and understanding of God. It reveals God's personal participation in every aspect of life. God is co-present, reveals Himself, and calls us to transcendence through human experience. Reality itself becomes the means to encounter and discover God, be it the predicaments of life, the desire for wholeness or the search for fulfilment, each in its own way points beyond us to the source of Life. In such moments we come to realise that God is present, real and active within us. For this reason experience is the instrumentality of knowing, responding to and participating in the reality of God. The way to God is to pay attention to our own experience and engage in critical reflection because this draws us into the recognition of a deeper reality and into another dimension of knowing and being.

Another Burning Bush?
The story of Moses and the burning bush can help us understand that our experience draws us into God's life just as the burning bush drew Moses into God's life. Moses' curiosity brought him to an encounter with God. Our instinct to know, to find answers, to make sense of life serves the same function. It brings us into contact with the ultimate and in this moment of encounter an irrevocable bond is established between God and ourselves. Just as with Moses, experience becomes a moment of dialogue, when the Transcendent Other reveals Himself as a personal God committed to humankind. In that encounter the reality that is God took on personal significance. For us, too, experience becomes the bridge to the personal discovery of God, to the knowledge of an intimate relationship, to a new level of unique, personal participation, to a new world of meaning and understanding. The self-communication of God changes the quality of our self-consciousness and self-understanding; it is always powerful and creative – it requires a personal response. One cannot become indifferent, whatever one's response. God was a reality that Moses had to experience for himself before he could know how close, intimate and involved this God was in his life. It was only then that he understood that God was always already there, always already caring and always already involved in his life. The experience of God generates the same convictions in us because this experience of Moses is replicated in our own lives. However, there

is one major difference, and that is the reality of the Incarnation. In Jesus we know without doubt the depth of God's commitment to us, His desire to share our lives completely and bring us to new life in this world and the next. The reality of the Incarnation is a much more explicit confirmation of Moses' experience and an even more profound invitation to know and share God's life. Through Jesus we know the 'already but not yet' of life in God.

The Power of Shared Experience

It is not enough to have an experience of God and discover its meaning and significance; we need others to help affirm the authenticity, meaning and truth of the experience. It is only when an experience is genuine that it can become insight and the basis for personal integration and growth. It is not always easy to interpret transcendent experiences. There is always the danger of a purely subjective interpretation that can lead to extravagant and fanciful rationalisations. We are always vulnerable to a merely psychological understanding of experience or a form of introspection unconnected with the reality of God. As important as experience of God is, it has to be confirmed and verified. This is an essential part of critical reflection. The great value of the Christian faith tradition is that it gives us language to describe and interpret transcendent experiences, and their significance beyond an individual's own personal experience, making possible a correlation between one's own experience and that of others. This process of validation helps clarify the experience and situate it within the faith tradition, so as to confirm that the same transcendent process is at work in us. It is impossible for individuals to assess their own experience without reference to the faith community. We depend on the collective wisdom of the faith community because 'individual experiences must be tried and tested against the corporate experiences of the community.'[9] It is only then that we have grounds to begin the process of spiritual integration. Applied spirituality recognises the need for people to undergo this process of validation. If, in the quest for meaning and insight, we can experience a connectedness with the wisdom of the past that is now affirmed and appropriated in our own experience, we have a better basis for deeper relationship and new spiritual integration.[10]

We cannot reduce the reality of God to the sum total of our experience or the accumulated wisdom of the community; neither is God an outgrowth of human need, to be confirmed or determined by human experience. However, since no single experience discloses the reality of God, we look to recurring experiences within the community to see if certain patterns emerge within the communal experience of God. In the light of this cumulative experience we judge the relevance and meaning of our individual transcendent experiences.[11] The value of such critical analysis not only gives us the opportunity to authenticate our experiences and add to the wisdom of the faith community, it also generates a personal sensitivity and receptivity to future experiences. Sharing these experiences is important because others, such as scripture scholars, theologians and the mystics, can reveal aspects of an experience we were not conscious of and thereby help us to grasp more fully the significance of the experience. We need others to help us discover God and ourselves.

The ability to grow through human experience toward a deeper understanding of the presence and activity of God helps us appreciate our beliefs – flesh them out so to speak – and give them a new birth in ourselves. Human experience then becomes a means through which we can appropriate and live our faith in a more vibrant and meaningful way. In the critical reflection on experience we discover the connection, and bridge the gap, between the theory and practice of faith. We can discover for ourselves how grace and nature co-operate and, most importantly, the correlation between the human experience of God and the gospel of Jesus.[12] Such discernment is a necessary quality in the practice of Christian discipleship because it reflects the movement away from mere conformity and uniformity of belief and practice to a way of being more in tune with the Spirit of God in everyday life.

More attention is now given to genuine, personal freedom that is the basis of an integrated spirituality, and there is more scope for the individual to be responsible for his or her faith commitment. Although the Church is the guardian and custodian of orthodoxy, and our spirituality needs to be rooted in and faithful to the tradition, discernment involves fostering spiritual growth by paying attention to one's unique history, experience, desires and feelings in relation to the signs of the times and the gospel message. We engage in discernment within a very specific context – that of the Christian ideal. The incarnation, life, death and resurrection of Jesus is a very powerful statement about who God is and what humankind is called to be. We are responsible for discovering and bringing to life the image of Christ that lies within us. This type of discernment is being advocated because it helps us accept the demands and responsibilities of discipleship in circumstances that are rapidly changing. Discernment puts us in touch with the Spirit of God who is present in these changes and who, through them, invites us to co-operate in the transformation of self and world into the image of God. There has to be a process of discernment that allows for a personally authentic response to relationship with God.

In this day and age we are aware of the dangers of individualism in which the individual is seen as more important than the common good. We know that if discernment tends to focus primarily on the self, then we neglect the necessary relationship and influence of the faith tradition and the wisdom of the community. While dialogue between community and the individual is important, it is also important that the lives of people are not so controlled and determined that they have no effective personal freedom in discernment. Discernment within a community of faith – being Christian – does not mean life in isolation, but being a member of a community. Christian discipleship is not primarily a private matter; it is first and foremost a response to God within the context of the believing community. Christianity is not a private affair between God and self; it also has an ecclesial and social dimension. Part of the process of discernment is our accountability not only to the faith tradition and self, but also to society. Since we are conscious of wanting to transform society in a manner that reflects Kingdom values, we need to consider the contribution our discernment will make to society. Discernment, then, is both an individual and a corporate activity; it helps to form our minds and hearts, and the traditions, values and practices that guide our life in God and each other. It is through the dialogue of discernment that we shape the community and the community shapes us. The good of the community must be a significant factor in all our choices. To try to find God's will in isolation can easily lead to delusion and disaster. Discerning the will of God, even in personal matters, is, in a real sense, both a corporate and a personal undertaking.

A Pointer to the Possible

The next step in the process of applied spirituality is the recognition that experience and discernment also call us beyond our present relationship with God and others through the transcendent ideals that emerge from of the process of discernment.[13] What has been learned and discovered has to be incorporated into our own spiritual living. Applied spirituality is a 'lived' spirituality in which transcendent ideals reveal the possibility of living more fully the inner reality of relatedness with God and the outer harmony of relationship with others. They help us to live in time and eternity, to live the communal life and the interior life.[14] These ideals facilitate the movement towards a more consonant relatedness with the Divine and the world; they move us beyond a passive participation to a more meaningful and dynamic encounter with the Divine.

Applied spirituality acknowledges the essential need of human life to discover and live in harmony with the mystery of God, and to be formed by, and give form to, those aspirations emerging from the transcendent experiences of human life. The experience of transcendence is the normal means through which we discover what we are uniquely called to be. Transcendence implies the possibility of being able to change, to grow, to move into a new awareness of relationship with God; it also implies a new type of knowing, and therefore makes possible a new depth of relationship. It has the capacity to reveal the deeper, hidden aspect of our lives and see self, others, events and things in the light of eternal reality. This desire and ability to encounter the Transcendent is the dominant dynamic of life. It is the means through which God draws us to Himself and gradually reveals the meaning and direction of life as it is meant to unfold in God. Transcendent ideals represent the invitation to make known and give concrete expression to the results of our experience and discernment.

These transcendent ideals are pointers to the possible. They guide the gradual unfolding of our life and express how our relationship with God might grow. These ideals need to be flexible because they are means, merely pointers, and not an end in themselves. We must be prepared to change and adapt when we encounter God in new experiences and new insights. An ideal implies that it is not attainable, that it can only be approximated. As such these ideals mobilise the best in us and lead us to the limits of our abilities. Ideals are meant to be temporary directives to guide us in our relationship with God in a way that takes into consideration our knowledge, limitations and unique calling. Flexibility, adaptability and docility to the Spirit characterise this willingness to be led by God since our ultimate fulfilment will not be found in the realisation of the ideals, but in the God who inspires them.

Abundant Life

The goal of an applied spirituality is to help ordinary people become aware of and understand their capacity for intimate, self-transcendent communion with a personal God.[15] Genuine religious experience engenders the sense of one's deepest self as an incarnated spirit responding with one's entire being to God. This is a sign and pointer of personal transformation in a God who infinitely transcends our existence, yet is intimately related to us; it is an experience of grace and the promise of redemption; we find ourselves standing in reverence and surrender toward a Being who is experienced as the Transcendent, Ultimate Ground of all. This transformation is never felt as a demand or intrusion. Rather, it is felt as an appeal to open the self to the love and activity of God, it is perceived as an invitation to intimate participation in God's life.

This experience generates sensitivity to God's presence and activity. It fosters an inner change of mind and heart, and promotes a new-found confidence and trust in God who invites us to such profound and real intimacy. On the path to such transcendent union we recover our deepest spiritual identity in God. As our relationship with God grows, we are aware of new horizons, previously unimagined possibilities; we acquire an enlightened vision of self, and others, as sharers in the love and power of God.

A consequence of this experience is the recognition that life and our earthly strivings can never satisfy our transcendent needs or help us achieve our ultimate destiny and true identity. We reach the point where we do not fear relinquishing those aspects of life that need to be changed. Neither do we live under the illusion that we can fulfil ourselves, nor believe that it is within our power to achieve ultimate self-actualisation without any sense of dependence upon God. It is precisely through the experience of God that we are freed from the illusion of self-sufficiency, and freed to acknowledge and accept our need of God. Divine grace opens us to the possibility of authentic transformation, integration and consonance; it frees us from the pursuit of anxious self-fulfilment. The experience of God does not deny our natural striving for fulfilment; rather it purifies and enhances it.

We tend to discover, sooner or later, that our own search for fulfilment cannot satisfy our ultimate needs. No degree of status or success or self-fulfilment can lead to self-realisation. These cannot fulfil all the potential of human personhood. This is not to denigrate success, competence or achievement in any of its forms. It is simply to point out that the fullest and richest experience of personhood can only be found in God. We find our true selves in God alone. No one can do for us what God can; no one can accomplish in us what God can. Encounter with God is meant to permeate one's entire life so that we experience within ourselves a movement away from trying to manufacture self to the realisation that God is the source of a wholeness and authenticity never imagined. This experience has a unique and comprehensive power to expand the concept of what it means to be human and, in the process, transform our lives. The experience of God reveals both our need and capacity for divinity. It validates the search for the divine. It introduces us to knowledge of God beyond reward or punishment. We experience ourselves participating in the love that is the origin of the universe and endowed with a sense of self that only God can give.

Something Old, Something New
We live in an age where 'there is little doubt that the centre of gravity in religion has shifted from authority to experience.'[16] This emphasis on experience indicates the movement toward the recovery of the transcendent dimension of experience and to an appreciation of existence as the immediate context of God's self-disclosure. Currently, we are at a decisive turning point in the life of the Church. Traditional thinking and the credibility of religious institutions are under tremendous pressure. There is a general suspicion regarding Church and doctrine. As we witness the decline of traditional religious practice and the uncertainty about belief, the effort to rediscover the essential truths and meaning becomes the responsibility of all Christians.[17] The movement away from sole reliance on doctrine and dogma creates the opportunity for all Christians to rediscover God in the reality of life. It is our common task, even as we critique former religious certainties and grieve for what has been lost, to identify, through dialogue and the variety of religious experience, the points of continuity between the past and the present. It is important that we preserve and incorporate the wisdom of former times as we try to inject a new vitality into the life of the Church and our spiritual living.

There is a new appreciation of the role and function of individual transcendent experience, within the context of the believing community. An individual's personal spirituality is seen as participating in and contributing to our shared, communal spirituality. Taking the Trinity as the model of unity and individuality, as the model of interrelationship and interaction, we share the burden and individual responsibility of implementing transcendent ideals, undertaking apostolic endeavours, sharing material goods, supporting the prophets and guiding those in search of God. We are Church in the way we are open to God speaking to and guiding His people. We believe in a God who is 'not the sum total of abstract divine attributes but rather a personal co-player in a divine drama, a living God of history who interacts with us through specific people, places, events, and who expects an answer from us in the here-and-now.'[18] This God who is transcendent and immanent, who participates in every aspect of life and history, who is found in the fulfilment of one's ordinary duties, in the service of the poor, in the moment when the divine meets human frailty and shares our woundedness, our doubts and joys. This God is as present in us as He is in the heart of creation.

This task may seem too difficult, but there is no other way. God has chosen to meet us in the reality of life. But we do not journey alone; we can depend on God completely and know that He is with us each step of the way. The journey is worth it because 'coming to know who we are is a lifetime or perhaps an eternal discovery, for we are created in the image of an infinite God who holds us in existence.'[19] We can only imagine who and what we really are, and look forward to the unfolding that only God can accomplish in us.

The Quest for the Kingdom

Part of this unfolding process is the realisation that we are meant to be agents of change and transformation not only for ourselves, but for the whole of creation. As we have seen, genuine spirituality can never be separated from life, just as the love of God cannot be separated from the love of neighbour. All humanity has the potential to reflect the divine because in Christ our humanity has undergone a fundamental transformation and an essential re-interpretation. From now on we will always be incomplete if we do not imitate the love, presence and reality of God. We cannot withhold the gift of self, just as God could not withhold the gift of himself; otherwise this would betray both God and life. An applied spirituality accepts the responsibility of living this truth, the truth that there is nothing or nobody alien to God or outside God's care and concern. To live the inner transformation begun in us by Christ entails not only a contemplative mode of being in the world, but also the responsibility to promote human fulfilment in and through the realisation of God's presence and activity in the world. The conviction and security of God's love is the source of the motivation for a conscious engaging in the world to make holy the everyday and the ordinary. The ethics of a genuine spirituality reach beyond the self to care for and facilitate the power and reality of God to transform all aspects of life.

It is our responsibility to establish the kingdom of God by living the wonder and power and presence of God in all dimensions of life. God's love challenges the way we live so that we cannot refuse to be wholeheartedly involved in expressing the reality of God present in us and the world. We realise that 'we do not have a relationship with God in addition to other relationships. We experience God and relate to God, in and through all our relationships. Our relationship with God is inseparable from every relationship we experience.'[20] It is inherent to relationship with God that we serve the genuine unfolding of authentic life, collaborate with others in building a better world and not withdraw from the joys, suffering or strivings of humanity. Neither do we wait passively for God to save us, or lift us up or love us – we are already saved and loved and lifted up. We live now understanding the part we play in co-creating the world with him, in sharing the salvation and redemption that is already ours. St Teresa of Avila recognised this proactive way of being Christian when she helped us understand that Christ has no body now on earth, no hands or feet or eyes but ours. God's presence is now in us.[21] In knowing the irrevocable, eternal bond that already exists between God and ourselves, and in the realisation that we really do imitate and continue the ministry of Jesus, we come to discover in ourselves and others our inherent dignity as sons and daughters of God called to mirror this fundamental truth. The quest to establish God's kingdom on earth reflects this and is the source of our desire that all people might experience this for themselves.

The Unexamined Life is Not Worth Living

Each generation is entrusted with the task of making real and applicable the faith it professes. As we engage in this process we do not want to reduce faith and spirituality to an idealistic interpretation or attempt to mitigate the reality of life and fall into the fantasy of pious platitudes. Although talking about faith and spirituality seems to have little currency in contemporary Western society, we are still confronted with the need to find significance and meaning for ourselves. If we fail to examine life then we condemn ourselves, as Thoreau suggested, to living lives of quiet desperation. We have no choice, then, except to enter into the stark facts of life. An applied spirituality helps us understand that reality is not removed from God, nor is God removed from reality. It also gives us a method of seeing and thinking about the mundane, the tragic and the mysterious in a way that tries to reveal their inner meaning and transcendent significance for everyday life. We have the opportunity to explore the people, events, and things of life from a faith perspective in order to discover for ourselves a God who is intimate, available and a real, participant presence in our lives.

Applied spirituality finds acceptable and credible the ordinary experiences of people to reveal knowledge and offer insights that guide us on our journey into God. When we do not appreciate the ordinary experiences of people we neglect the wisdom that is just beyond an open mind and a willing heart. Many an experience, idea or insight has died a lonely death because it was not shared and appreciated, it fade into mere anecdote unless it is identified, named, described, interpreted and shared. An applied spirituality acknowledges the need for experiences to be critically evaluated so that they may be debunked as irrelevant or tweaked into greater significance. Either way, we are the richer for taking human experiences seriously.

We must also acknowledge that people may consciously or unconsciously resist the notion of an applied spirituality. The reason being that it challenges us to new ways of seeing and thinking about life. If we engage in this type of critical reflection it is paramount to expressing a desire to change and grow beyond where we are now. This kind of reflection will create an uncomfortable and untenable existence for us in the sense that we will inevitably be challenged to change and grow, and even be transformed in ways beyond our wildest imaginings. Thus, applied spirituality is an art, an invitation to evaluate and examine the experiences of life. It echoes a deep appreciation of what Plato meant when he declared that the unexamined life was not worth living.

Notes

1   M. Frohlich, 'Spiritual Discipline, Discipline of Spirituality', *Spiritus: A Journal of Christian Spirituality, Vol. 1, #1.* (2001) 75-76.

2   K. Waaijman, *Spirituality: Forms, Foundations, Methods,* Trans. John Vriend., (Leuven: Peeters, 2002), 364.

3   M. Downey, *Understanding Christian Spirituality,* (New York: Paulist Press, 1997) 31.

4   K. Rahner, *The Practice of Faith: A Handbook of Contemporary Spirituality,* (New York: Crossroads: 1992) 62-68.

5   See D. Lane's book, *The Experience of God: An Invitation to do Theology,* (Dublin: Veritas, 2003) for an overview of current thinking about the role and function of experience.

6   Ibid., 23.

7   Ibid., 17.

8   John Paul II, *Redemptor Hominis,* (1979) n. 18.

9   D. Lane, *The Experience of God,* 22.

10   Ibid., 16.

11   Ibid., 17.

12   Ibid., 17.

13   A. Van Kaam, *Fundamental Formation: Formative Spirituality, Vol. 1.* (New York: Crossroads, 1983) 169-177.

14   M. Frohlich, 'Spiritual Discipline, Discipline of Spirituality', 74.

15   Ibid., 74.

16   D. Lane, *The Experience of God,* 26.

17   P. Sheldrake, 'The Crisis of Postmodernity', *Christian Spirituality Bulletin, Vol. 4, #1, Summer* 1996, 6-10.

18   A. W. Astell, 'Postmodern Christian Spirituality: A Coincidentia Oppositorum?' (*Christian Spirituality Bulletin, Vol. 4, #1, Summer* 1996) 4.

19   C. M. Kelly, *Symbols of Inner Truth: Uncovering the Spiritual Meaning of Experience.* (New York: Paulist Press, 1988) 19-20

20   D. O'Leary, *Passion for the Possible: A Spirituality of Hope for a New Millenium,* (Dublin, Columba Press, 1998) 19.

21   Ibid., 17.

Seeking God in All Things: Ignatian Spirituality as Action Research[1]

Dr David Coghlan SJ

The Ignatian approach to spirituality views God as active in the world, inviting us to ever closer collaboration. God can be sought and found in our own experience. The Ignatian God is a busy God, and is to be found not – or at least not only – in some static bliss, but rather in acting, in creating.[2] In the Contemplation for Learning to Love Like God, found at the end of the Spiritual Exercises, we pray to find God in the gifts of our world and in how God 'works and labours' for me (*Spiritual Exercises* 236). We seek to love as God loves – and, since love is expressed in action (*Spiritual Exercises* 230), this means we seek to act as God acts, responding according to the grace we receive. In Ignatian spirituality there is an integral link between prayer and activity. Ignatius offers us a structured set of methods for developing the interaction between the two.

It could be said, therefore, that Ignatian spirituality promotes a form of what is now known as *action research*. This term is used in the world of the social sciences – social work, community development, organisation development, nursing, management and so on – to denote an approach to research that integrates the inquiry proper to research with ongoing action. People typically present action and reflection as occurring in a cycle: one moves from planning to the action itself, to evaluation, and then to planning something new.[3] We learn from our reflection on experience. Knowledge and action are organically connected: knowledge is generated through reflection in and on action.

In recent years, social science researchers have come to recognise the close connections between knowledge and action. In this context, they have also come to acknowledge the value of spirituality. Recent contributions to the literature have commended a simple awareness of the sacred,[4] transpersonal forms of spirituality,[5] and the Buddhist emphasis on mindful inquiry.[6] But perhaps they have not yet fully recognised the potential of mainstream Christianity.

In this article, I shall try to redress the balance by pointing to some striking overlaps between motifs of Ignatian spirituality – a spirituality in which 'action' is a central motif – and the features of this new pattern of thinking in the social sciences known as action research. Action research is having an increasing influence on the study of spirituality, particularly in its applied forms, and it may be both useful and timely to draw out its similarities to at least one major school of Christian spirituality. Moreover, the technical concepts developed by action research theory might help sharpen the processes of reflection encouraged by Ignatian spirituality. Though the methods of the social sciences are sometimes reductive, either bracketing the religious or else translating it into other – allegedly more accurate – terms, the processes of action research are quite appropriate to the knowledge born of grace and of religious faith.

What is Action Research?

The word 'research' is associated in most people's minds with ideas, with theories. Research is conducted in the world of ideas and their formulation. It was this standard, seemingly common-sense notion of research that shaped the development of the social sciences. Research, on this model, examines an 'objective' truth, which exists outside the world of the researcher and which is disconnected from the action of everyday life. Research techniques were thus concerned with objective impartiality, with forms of knowledge that were 'valid' and that applied universally.

Social science no longer works with this model alone. When postmodernism began to emerge some thirty years ago, people became more aware of language, and in particular of how our experience is influenced as much by the language we use as by any 'objective' reality. Others have come to regard the purpose of human inquiry not simply as the creation of knowledge for itself, but rather the *enhancement of good practice* in everyday life. The knowledge sought contributes to relationships, to aesthetics, to ecology and to human flourishing.[7] Now, it is argued, is a time for science *in* action rather than science *about* action.

It is in this context that the idea of 'action research' has come to the fore. In the words of two of its leading advocates, action research aims,

> ... to forge a more direct link between intellectual knowledge and moment to moment personal and social action, so that inquiry contributes directly to the flourishing of human persons, their communities and the ecosystems of which they are part.[8]

Action research has roots in the work of Kurt Lewin, one of the founding fathers of social psychology; in Paolo Freire's work on consciousness-raising; and in various schools of liberation thought, notably Marxist and feminist. We can identify four central characteristics:

- a focus on practical issues, aiming to produce knowledge-in-action
- a participatory mode of doing research *with* people rather than *on* people
- an awareness that truth emerges over time, and that the process may be as important as the outcome
- a concern that new knowledge should lead people into a dynamic of emancipation.[9]

Ignatian Sources

Ignatius, as is well known, spoke of finding God in all things. His close confidant, Jerómino Nadal, who did much to disseminate Ignatian teaching among the early Jesuits, once described Ignatius as 'contemplative in action', and developed a sustained doctrine of the circle of prayer and action. He spoke of the necessity 'of returning often to prayer and of realising a circular movement passing from prayer to action and from action back to prayer'. In a recent discussion of these ideas, Peter-Hans Kolvenbach, the current Jesuit General, points out that Nadal's cycle does not imply two different, competing realities, one of which would detract from the other. Rather, people following this path are to be penetrated by 'the one divine grace'. Kolvenbach then develops the idea:

> Keeping the image of the cycle, one might say that, in the spiritual progression of the apostolic life, the circle ceaselessly contracts until the two components – prayer and action – mutually

penetrate in a harmony by which our human activity becomes the activity of God within us.

The whole reality of human existence becomes the setting where God's action reveals itself. [10]

In these ideas we find remarkable convergences with action research. Action research does not recognise the distinction between theory and action in the way that traditional social science research does. Rather it reflects Kurt Lewin's maxim that there should be no theory without action and no action without theory.

The central dynamic of action research is the enactment of cycles of reflection and action, where the development is from reflection *about* action to critical inquiry *in* action, aiming at 'timely, voluntary, mutual, validity-testing, transformative action at all moments of living'.[11] Clearly there are theological convictions underlying the Ignatian vision which theorists of action research do not express and to which they may well not subscribe. For Christians formed in the Ignatian tradition, the reflection in question here is an inquiry into how God is at work in their lives and in the world, and into how God might shape appropriate responses and reactions for here and now. But both Ignatian spirituality and action research involve a close integration of action and reflection. Just as believers may find that Ignatian spirituality enables a full theological understanding of the processes of action research, so the concepts and ideas developed in action research theory may well enrich and sharpen our understanding of what happens in Ignatian reflection, indeed in an everyday examen. I propose to introduce various other ideas from action research theory, and to show how this enrichment and sharpening might take place.

Forms of Knowing

Action research theory sometimes distinguishes four kinds of knowing, reflecting different ways in which we deal with and act within the world:

- *Experiential knowing*: the knowledge arising as we encounter the realities around us
- *Presentational knowing*: the knowledge expressed in our giving form to this experiential knowing, through language, images, music, painting and the like
- *Propositional knowing*: the knowledge distilling our experiential and presentational knowing into theories, statements and propositions

- *Practical knowing*: the knowledge that brings the other three forms of knowing to full fruition by *doing* appropriate things, skilfully and competently.[12]

This scheme of four kinds of knowing – experience, expression, understanding, practice – can be applied to our relations with God. What for the Christian is the knowledge born of faith and prayer (*experiential* knowing) is expressed in *presentational* form through our images of God, through the language of our prayers, through religious art and music. That experiential and presentational knowing is articulated in *propositional* form in the statements of our faith, in the Creed, in how our beliefs are formulated and understood through theology. All this is expressed in *practical* knowing as we apply ourselves to trying to live the Christian faith. In terms of the Exercises, these forms of knowing involve attending to our experience of a personal God, who sent the Son to redeem us and who invites us to love in the way that God loves and to serve God in the world. It means attending to how that love shapes our experience, to how we express and try to understand it and to how it guides our living and acting in the world.[13]

Phases

Action research also typically distinguishes between four phases in human projects:

- *Intentions*: purpose, goals, aims and vision
- *Planning*: plans, strategy, tactics, schemes
- *Action*: implementation, performance
- *Outcomes*: results, consequences and effects.[14]

Action research aims to develop our awareness, understanding and skills across all these phases. We try to understand our intentions, to develop appropriate plans and strategies, to be skilled at carrying them out, to reflect on how well we have carried them out, and to evaluate their results. We can also inquire about the connections between these phases. We might, for example, begin with the outcomes, and explore how our actions caused these outcomes. Or we may take the inquiry further, and look at how our intentions and plans shaped our actions.

Ignatian spirituality encourages us to reflect in the same kind of way. The Exercises are concerned above all with 'what I want and desire' (*Spiritual Exercises*, 48.1) and with how these desires lead us to act in co-operation with God. The reflection on experience characteristic of Ignatian spirituality typically encourages us to become aware of how our behaviour and its results are rooted in our intentions and desires.

Audiences

Perhaps, however, the most helpful contribution that action research theory can make to Ignatian spirituality comes from the idea that an integrative approach to research incorporates three different *audiences*, which are called 'first person', 'second person' and 'third person'.[15] First person inquiry-practice centres on what is happening for the individual researcher. Second person inquiry-practice focuses on the quality of relationships the researcher forms. Third person inquiry-practice disseminates the research to the wider impersonal community.

The classical methods of research worked with 'third person' procedures: a researcher did research on third persons and wrote a report for other third persons. Postmodern theory introduced 'second person' procedures: researchers became aware of their 'positionality', of how their observation itself involved them in the reality being observed. Action research, however, involves all three audiences, all three voices.

First Person Inquiry-Practice

First person inquiry-practice is typically characterised as the form of inquiry-practice that one does on one's own. It fosters the individual's ability to develop an inquiring approach to their own life, and to act in ways that are informed, aware and purposeful. First person inquiry can take us 'upstream', when we inquire into our basic assumptions, desires, intentions and philosophy of life. It can also take us 'downstream', when we inquire into our behaviour, ways of relating, and action in the world. First person inquiry-practice typically finds expression in autobiographical writing: diaries, journals, records of dreams and so on. It also occurs through meditation and prayer.

Ignatius' *Autobiography* well illustrates first person inquiry-practice. Experience was the main catalyst of change in his life.[16] As Ignatius reflected on his experiences he saw the patterns of God's action, and that insight directed him to future action. Throughout his life he knew how he was subjected to different ways of being stirred to act. He devoted a lot of attention to finding out what moved him in each situation and what kind of action the movement was leading to. He became a master of discernment: he learnt to distinguish and clarify his motivations and the reasons behind his judgements, to probe the causes and implications of what he had experienced, and to weigh and evaluate the likely consequences of the alternatives before him in order to discover what would best lead to the desired goal. For instance, his accounts of the movements of his spirit while on his sickbed in Loyola illustrate both his attention to his moods and his sense of how God was leading him.

Whenever individuals seek to find God in their lives, they are undertaking first person research. This form of inquiry involves seeking God both in times of prayer and in the events of daily life. The *Spiritual Exercises* articulate the process more fully. We discover and acknowledge sin, both our own sin and the world's social sin. We learn that we are nevertheless forgiven, and become desirous to respond to Christ's call, a call to 'love and serve in all things'. Spiritual development occurs in the events of everyday life as the individual attends to experience, makes judgements and assumes responsibility for actions. The whole process occurs within the context of a growing conversion to God's loving action in the world.

A vivid example of first person inquiry is to be found in a reflective essay by Timothy Toohig, a Jesuit physicist who died in 2001.[17] Drawing on Karl Rahner's thought, Toohig views his physics as a deeper penetration into the mystery of creation, and he therefore regards research in physics as praise of God. He uses two words to capture the integration of his physics research and his spirituality: 'honesty' as he confronts the data; and 'authenticity' as he acknowledges the mystery. Honesty and authenticity colour his whole life, not just his physics.

The Ignatian examen, too, can be seen as a paradigm of first person inquiry. We recall the experiences of the day; we notice our responses and probe what was happening within us, what God might have been telling us in a particular incident; we wonder about what we might do next – whether to repent, to give thanks, or to take some further action.[18] We look not only at the immediate details, but also at their motivational roots. The process moves freely between the two: 'upstream' from action to motivation, and 'downstream' from reflection to thoughts of doing something new.

Second Person Inquiry-Practice

Second person inquiry-practice occurs as we inquire with others into issues of mutual concern, through face-to-face dialogue and conversation.

A clear example of second person inquiry-practice in Ignatius' lifetime can be found in the 1539 formal deliberation that occurred when Ignatius and his companions came together to discern what God wanted of them, and in particular whether they should constitute themselves as a permanent group.[19] During the Deliberation, the companions engaged in first person prayer and meditation and then in second person sharing. Over a period of time they lived through questions and uncertainties, exploring the advantages and disadvantages of particular options until they reached unanimity. The outcome was the foundation of the Society of Jesus.

A Christian living in the spirit of Ignatius will be involved in second person inquiry-practice by virtue of their being engaged in a community of faith, whether it be formally in religious life, or in something like a Christian Life Community group, or in an informal network of friends which meets to share faith and support its members. In such contexts individuals share something of their own first person inquiry while the others listen. Then the group attempts to draw together its sense of where God is leading the group. Any form of discernment in common involves second person inquiry-practice.

Second person inquiry-practice also takes place in spiritual direction. The individual and their spiritual director engage in conversation about the individual's life-experience and about how they are seeking to find God in it. Second person inquiry-practice may also find expression in task-oriented teamwork, where the team's purpose, the means of achieving it, the team's procedures, and the development of the individual can all be understood in Ignatian terms.[20]

Third Person Inquiry-Practice

Third person inquiry-practice also takes place within a community of inquiry. But here the bonds are more impersonal, going beyond the kind of contact fostered by direct mutual collaboration. It involves reporting, publishing, and extrapolating from the concrete to the general.

Ignatius' *Spiritual Exercises*, his *Constitutions of the Society of Jesus*, and many of his letters illustrate third person inquiry-practice. His own experience in personal and interpersonal settings is presented in a form that can be taken up by others whom he has never met. The contact becomes impersonal. In the Christian life more generally, third person inquiry-practice becomes visible in the corporate life of the Church, and in the progress of the planet as a whole. We try to help build up communities of faith; we seek to promote God's action in the world at the institutional and structural levels. Much writing and teaching in Ignatian spirituality centres on theology, on instruction on spirituality, on the promotion of justice, on pedagogy, on organisational processes[21] and the like. This material expresses third person inquiry-practice.

The Three Audiences

In terms of action research, therefore, we can see Ignatian spirituality as involving all three styles of inquiry-practice, all three audiences. We begin with a first person response to the Call of the King, the Two Standards and the Contemplation for Learning to Love Like God, rooted in the individual's enquiry about how God is found in their experience. We then engage in second person inquiry with others who are living their Christian life in particular circumstances. Finally, this may bear fruit in a wisdom articulated impersonally, in structural and institutional terms – in other words, in third person inquiry-practice. All these processes require us to attend to the different forms and phases of knowing mentioned above, as they are informed by our religious faith, and as our knowledge is discerned and confirmed through action.

Converging Traditions

Ignatian cycles of prayer and action find an echo in the cycles of action and reflection articulated in action research theory. Action research works with a richer and more differentiated account of knowledge than those implicit in more classical models of social science, and can therefore accommodate the Ignatian conviction that our prayer and action are grounded in grace, in the reality of being in love with God. The framework of first, second and third person forms of inquiry-practice can yield helpful insight both into Ignatius' own life and into the life of a contemporary Christian.

The worlds of Ignatian spirituality and the world of social research have not often been in close contact. Yet there are many who have been transformed by the Exercises and who live out of a spirituality which can be termed Ignatian – people whose commitment to seeking God in all things leads them to a cycle of action within the world, to reflection, and to prayer. This Ignatian commitment may well be nourished and enhanced by the rigorous methods of action research. For social science itself is now moving towards a concern for action. It is coming to see itself as actively responding to reality, as committed to creating a more meaningful and just world. And thus it has begun to acknowledge and draw on the spirituality of individuals and groups who engage in such action. If the two traditions can converse and cross-fertilise, the fruit may well be both abundant and rich.

Notes

1 This article appeared in *The Way* in January 2004.
2 D. L. Fleming, 'Finding a Busy God', in *A Spirituality for Contemporary Life* (St Louis: Review for Religious, 1991) 21-30.
3 D. Coghlan and Teresa Brannick, *Doing Action Research in Your Own Organization* (London: Sage, 2001).
4 P. Reason, 'Reflections on Sacred Experience and Sacred Science', *Journal of Management Inquiry*, 2/3 (1993) 273-283.
5 J. Heron, 'Transpersonal Cooperative Inquiry', in *Handbook of Action Research: Participative Inquiry and Practice*, edited by P. Reason and H. Bradbury (London: Sage, 2001) 333-339.
6 V. Malhotra Bentz and Jeremy J. Shapiro, *Mindful Inquiry in Social Research* (Thousand Oaks, Ca: Sage, 1997).
7 P. Reason and J. Rowan (eds.), *Human Inquiry: A Sourcebook of New Paradigm Research*, (Chichester: Wiley, 1981); Reason and Bradbury, *Handbook of Action Research*.
8 P. Reason and W. R. Torbert, 'The Action Turn: Toward a Transformational Social Science', *Concepts and Transformation*, 6/1 (2001) 1-37, at 6.
9 This classification draws on Reason and Bradbury, *Handbook of Action Research*, 2.
10 The immediate source for this paragraph is P. H. Kolvenbach, 'On the Effectiveness of the Spiritual Exercises', written for the Ignatian centenary in 1991 and reproduced in *The Road from La Storta*, edited by C. F. Starkloff, (St Louis Institute of Jesuit Resources, 2000) 189-199 at 196-197. Fuller references and background are to be found in E. Coreth, 'Contemplation in Action' (1954) in *Contemporary Spirituality*, edited by R. W. Gleason (New York: Macmillan, 1968) 184-211; R. Hostie, 'The Circle of Prayer and Action' (1955) in *Finding God in All Things*, translated by W. J. Young (Chicago: Regnery, 1958) 153-165; P. Endean, *Karl Rahner and Ignatian Spirituality* (Oxford: OUP, 2001) 68-93.
11 Reason and Torbert, 'The Action Turn', 6.
12 Ibid., 13.
13 T. Dunne, 'Spiritual Integration in Ignatius of Loyola', *Review for Religious*, 45 (1986) 856-869.
14 Reason and Torbert, 'The Action Turn', 14.
15 Reason and Bradbury, *Handbook of Action Research*, 14.
16 D. Lonsdale, *Eyes to See, Ears to Hear: An Introduction to Ignatian Spirituality* (London: Darton, Longman and Todd, 2000 [1991]).
17 T. E. Toohig, 'Physics Research: A Search for God', *Studies in the Spirituality of Jesuits*, 21/2 (March 1999).
18 See, for example, J. A. Tetlow, 'The Examen of Particulars', *Review for Religious*, 56 (1997) 230-250 at 248-250.
19 See J. J. Toner, 'The Deliberation that Started the Jesuits', *Studies in the Spirituality of Jesuits*, 6/4 (September 1974).
20 D. Coghlan, 'Ignatian Teamwork: An Emergent Framework from the Instructions for the Team at Trent', *Review of Ignatian Spirituality*, no. 98 (2001) 65-74.
21 D. Coghlan, *Good Instruments: Ignatian Spirituality, Organisation Development and the Renewal of Ministries* (Rome: CIS, 1999).

Gender and Spiritual Guidance in Postmodern[1] Contexts

Dr Jack Finnegan SDB

In the light of the Incarnation, spirituality is undoubtedly concerned with how to live in the complex world of events.

Philip Sheldrake[2]

Culture and spirituality meet in the paradox of gender and the range of concerns that centre on it. These concerns lie at the heart of contemporary experience and have immediate implications for male dominated hierarchical structures in both ecclesial and civil life.[3] Here, my hypothesis is that gender issues both influence and are influenced by the interplay of socio-cultural and religious processes, practices, and concepts and are encountered within contemporary spiritual guidance relationships. I further hypothesise that the perceived distinctions between *sexuality* and *gender* have a significant influence on the perceptions and expectations of those who offer and receive spiritual guidance.[4] These expectations and perceptions in turn influence the structure of identity. The largely unconscious nature of these forces gives pause for thought. It becomes the ground for reflection and informed debate on a range of cognate issues in both applied spirituality and spiritual guidance, theory and practice.

I describe spiritual guidance, or spiritual direction, as a caring, discerning, helping, supporting, tutoring, and transformative activity. It focuses on the implications of spirituality in a person's life, in a relational context that has both contemplative-charismatic and skill-based professional dimensions. It does this, according to Elizabeth Liebert, by eliciting from the partners in the guidance relationship a specific sensitivity to divine action characterised as 'particular modes of seeing, hearing, naming, responding, celebrating and acting.'[5] The spiritual guidance relationship is usually characterised by a spiritual or theological tradition. This point is well made by Kenneth Leech when he portrays spiritual direction as 'a relationship of friendship in Christ between two people by which one is enabled, through the personal encounter, to discern more clearly the will of God for one's life, and to grow in discipleship and the life of grace.'[6] As Philip Sheldrake so succinctly puts it, at 'the heart of Christian theology, and therefore spirituality, is an invitation to enter a new world.'[7] Spirituality in this sense may be likened to a life-long journey characterised by recognisable encounters with God in the daily realities of life.[8] I draw attention to the relativism characteristic of postmodern philosophies of knowledge.[9]

I also draw attention to the centrality of language where even science is viewed as just one more language game.[10] This turn to language offers a potential spiritual and theological opportunity if only because it correlates with the foundational Johannine assertion (Jn 1:1). The postmodern milieu challenges us to face the problems raised by linguistic totalism, according to which every experience is radically structured by the language of our human community. While the relativism espoused by postmodernity causes serious problems for truth claims and the validity of meta-narratives – the Bible is an example – it does allow us to take Christian theological and spiritual language seriously in local cultural context. In such relativised cultural contexts Christian authenticity becomes a grounding responsibility for those who share the Christian story. The Christian voice needs to be convincingly present in the postmodern milieu. It has pertinent things to offer on a range of issues, not least on vital cosmic, economic and moral challenges. The implication is that spiritual and practical theologies need to be philosophical enough to enter into the public discourse of a pluralistic society, prepared to give public reasons for their practical proposals.[11]

Gender

We turn now to the core theme of gender as it impacts on and is encountered in the spiritual guidance context. Let me surface a number of initial questions:

- Do women and men experience the giving and receiving of spiritual guidance in the same ways?
- Are processes of gender stereotyping and discrimination to be found in the practices and policies that underpin the provision and practice of spiritual guidance?

- Are gender assumptions, contrasexual projections, and assumptions of gender normativity left unrecognised and undisturbed in spiritual guidance practice and training?
- To what extent has spiritual guidance practice been scrutinised for male bias or gender blindness?
- How well are issues of *parataxic distortion* recognised in spiritual guidance practice and training?[12]
- Are issues of differential treatment, particularly those that are rooted in gender prejudice and bias, discussed and identified, and are the potentially abusive consequences of differential treatment – unthinking at best and oppressive at worst – understood?
- Have marginalising forces been accurately identified?
- Have issues of equal access been identified?
- Borrowing from the world of education, has the covert gender curriculum been identified and made evident in spiritual guidance practice and training?
- What role does qualified supervision play in the identification and development of best practice in this formidable context?

Why should gender issues be raised in the context of the practice of spiritual guidance? Like other areas concerned with justice and the quest for liberating transformation, gender questions must be faced for at least two reasons. The first is to ensure that spiritual guidance practice does no harm. The second is to ensure that spiritual guidance practice survives and develops as a meaningful liberating, transformative activity in the realities of contemporary life. To do this honestly a clear understanding of sexual and gender-based subordination processes and structures of discrimination and their impact on human identity needs to be put in place.[13] Knowingly and unknowingly, cultural hierarchies, the forces of defensive splitting, and heterosexist bias continue to assert powerful influence on practitioners and trainers alike.[14] Spiritual theology in general and spiritual practice in particular must acknowledge the inextricability of sexual and economic subordination in the lives of many. This is usually a product of gender stereotyping and consequent gender injustice.

Other questions suggest themselves. What has spiritual theology to say in the lives of women trapped in violent marriages or forced into prostitution? What has it to say to the many whose gender difference or fear disturbs complacently held male dominated status quo biases? What has it to say to those subjected to homophobic violence? More significantly, what has it to say to the victims of political or ecclesial marginalisation, especially when it is rooted in what Sarah Coakley describes as 'the insidious entanglements of gender with race, class and other factors of discrimination in the hierarchy of oppressions'?[15] To what extent do mainstream (malestream?) theologies, which usually inform spiritual guidance practices and training, need to recognise that there is really no such thing as asexual, non-contextual or ahistorical theology?[16] Spiritual guidance practitioners need to reflect deeply on the relevance of Christian theology to sexual minorities, to lesbian, gay, bisexual, and transsexual persons. Fifteen years ago Steven Connor drew attention to 'patriarchy's Other, identified with the dark and discredited side of every polarity, as body to mind, nature to culture, night to day, matter to form and madness to reason.'[17] The spiritual guidance practitioner is invited to explore these dark margins and discern the Divine Other in them.

This surfaces another significant hypothesis concerning the nature of communication. The assumption that persons are capable of making their own interests clear results in a strongly narrative emphasis in spiritual guidance. However, this emphasis presumes a range of shared literacies.[18] Hermeneutical theory suggests that all communication is distorted to some extent by fundamental pre-understandings of which the parties in the spiritual guidance relationship tend to be unaware. We know from depth psychology that a person's most powerful motivations are those most likely to be repressed. The implication is that language does not directly reflect experience given the complex range of influences that are at work.[19] Again, feelings don't just occur in relation to objects of cognition.[20] Objects of cognition themselves occur in relation to wider, complex and often politicised social systems, particularly educational and economic systems, that ultimately condition our experiential narratives. The complex nature of communication raises a crucial question for those engaging in spiritual guidance. In what sort of space does spiritual guidance take place? What else is going on in the room, in the people concerned? What presences and influences are at work? How possible is it for spiritual guidance to take place in an arena of pure interiority, free from the influence of a multiplicity of inner and outer forces and stimuli? Herein lies the contemplative challenge: attending to the Divine in the messiness of the lived experience of real people in real life contexts.

The Gendered Subject

The term *gendered subject* implies that to be a subject one must be gendered. How does this happen? Unfortunately for the spiritual guidance practitioner the contemporary answer to this question is complex and contested. As Polly Young-Eisendrath points out, biological theories of masculinity and femininity have been undermined in feminist and linguistic debates, as well as by work in psychoanalysis and sociology.[21] In contemporary society there seems to be no straightforward answer to what constitutes and shapes the human person as a gendered, or indeed, embodied subject. Such factors as systems of ideas and reiterative and performative social dynamics are held to play an influential role. The repetition of gender norms is understood to both animate and constrain the gendered subject. From this point of view, gender is understood to be a socio-cultural, rather than a natural, category. Judith Butler, a leading postmodern theorist, claims that both sex and gender are products of 'regulatory fictions that consolidate and naturalise the convergent power regimes of masculine and heterosexist oppression.'[22] From a spiritual point of view the implied transcendence of nature in such a theory is fascinating.[23] The same is held to be true of our body images. According to Harvie Ferguson, the body image itself emerges as a social reality through a continuous process of self-creation. It realises itself in and through the habitual psychic make-up of people in live interactions. Resulting from the interaction of such social mechanisms as identification, imitation, and projection, body image plays a significant role in the construction of contemporary identity.[24]

It would appear that these are also the resources from which identity and gender resistance, subversion, and displacement are forged. The point here concerns the performative force of language itself as it draws the gendered subject towards conformity with normative socio-cultural or ethical models.[25] It is important for spiritual guidance practitioners to recognise the forces at work when gendered identity is destabilised. This occurs when strongly held prevailing assumptions and reliance on a particular conceptual system are overthrown, as is the case in certain contemplative mystical experiences. This gives rise to an important question for the spiritual or pastoral practitioner. What happens when spiritual experience subverts conventional gender assumptions? What happens when the normative models of gender identification not only disturb but also terrify the gendered subject? What do you do when confronted with the anxiety of a person who encounters intense spiritual desire itself as a threat, particularly when it spills over into sexual experience? As Judy Norton points out, gendered subjectivities have the capacity to express social meanings, but they also have the capacity to precipitate concrete social consequences.[26] The implications are hugely significant.

Psychoanalyst Susan Fairfield recognises that where matters of gender and sexuality are concerned clinical work reflects larger societal biases and their potential for harm when they are unthinkingly restated in therapeutic contexts.[27] Spiritual guidance practitioners run the same risk. The gendered subject does not exist in a vacuum, but is open to a range of influences, including both masculinist and feminist standpoints.[28] Whatever else the spiritual practitioner may bring to this discourse, the principle of gender justice must play a cardinal role. How safe is it in practice to assume shared understandings about the nature of women and men? It is evident that most people develop an implicit theory, a naive psychology, or some sort of cognitive representation of gender and gender differences. These cognitive structures are summaries of a person's experience and are presented in the linguistic and cultural forms available to the narrator. They serve as filters that modify an individual's own perceptions and behaviours.[29] Gender role self-perceptions underlie attitudes, beliefs, and behaviours and colour interaction and communication with others. We see the gendered subject rather than the real person and thereby risk projective entanglement. Encountering real persons as gendered subjects frequently confronts the spiritual practitioner with the phenomenon of the lessened, impoverished, diminished, and distanced Other. Is there anyone real beyond the perceived gendered subject? Is the encounter largely a theatre of projections and linguistic performance?[30] Unfortunately, in the spaces where perceptions and ideologies interact with social structures the real person often disappears and becomes invisible.[31]

Gender identity becomes second nature to us, a form of habitus, because it names a deeply rooted, bodily anchored dimension of life. It affects the individual in the parts of personal identity experienced as most natural. It raises concerns about a person's body, the vision of the body, the possibilities of sensual perception, and significantly for spiritual guidance practice, of feeling and the capacity to express pleasure and pain.[32] Socially, gender is linked to a wide range of cognate themes. As well as race and ethnicity, these include ageism, sexual orientation, disability, alternative identities, the reality of ecological devastation, and a slew of justice issues. The combining of these elements in a single list is deliberate; each names contexts in which the risk of the erasure of everything unique and distinct is real. Further, the linkage between the core themes of sexuality, gender, and identity is subject to what Michel Foucault terms 'polymorphous techniques of power'.[33] Culture has the power not only to strengthen the feelings of belonging in some, but also to increase the feelings of exclusion in others.[34] Exclusion should be easy enough for the experienced spiritual practitioner to recognise. It is more difficult to break free of the tendency to simply ignore what is different and disturbing, and to refuse to acknowledge how damaging it is to evade particular distinctiveness in favour of the generic and the universal. Neat theories make fine bunkers.

The honest practitioner needs to be alert to a range of operative dangers in these contexts. These include the danger posed by unawareness of the practitioner's own cultural location and the spiritual, religious, or theological influences on gender assumptions that arise from it. Gender cannot be taken for granted. What else is blocked when something so foundational is ignored? What awareness of otherness may not say itself? What awareness is silenced? The practitioner also needs to ponder the extent to which gender inequalities point to other inequalities. Professor Lynne Layton points out that despite all the evidence 'of gender multiplicity and fluidity ... each of us, no matter what our race, class, or sexuality, contends in some way psychically with dominant gender, race, class, and sexual categories, because the dominant categories hold the power to define what proper race, class, gender, and sexuality is.'[35]

In caring contexts meaning itself may be experienced as a site of multi-layered complexity especially because it involves the encounter with the Other in spaces that seem alike and familiar. The contribution of post-structural theory is useful here because it modifies the horizon against which these issues are viewed. Post-structuralism rejects the presence of over-arching structures in social life. It argues for fragmentation and diversity in social life. In this way it challenges the way we understand the relationship between human beings, their culture, and the world.[36] While culture invests us with agency and choice, it also limits the possibilities on offer. But if the cultural script is not fixed, we can intervene to increase the range of options. Transformation becomes feasible. Hence the need for delicacy of touch and word when we are privileged to witness the unfolding mystery of

Spirit in another. Words do not unproblematically reflect the world. The way we live our lives in society, the constraints and empowerments that operate, take effect in language. Think of what this means in terms of the in-breaking Spirit and experiences that defy both language and reason.

Gender Studies

It is important for the spiritual guidance practitioner to be aware of the wide range of issues subsumed under the heading of Gender Studies. Gender Studies addresses such topics as the acquisition of gender identity across cultures; the influence of gender upon spirituality, moral choice, creativity, and language use; the relationship of gender to a wide spectrum of social problems such as poverty and violence; the history of various gender-related issues such as family life, marriage, reproduction, divorce, childrearing, sexual behaviour, sexual orientation, gender socialisation; men, women and friendship; men, women and romance; gender and communication; gender and language; gender and the media; gender and morality; gender and economics; gender and ways of knowing, and the like. It also pays attention to such significant factors as violence against women, the men's movement, contemporary theories of love and relationships, queer theory, sexual abuse, and lesbian, gay, bisexual and transsexual issues. What needs to be understood is that, despite claims to the contrary, at present sexual orientation is not a well-defined concept. Spiritual guidance practitioners ought to be alert to this lack of agreement and the difficulties experts encounter in developing accurate measures of orientation.[37] It is worth noting that in some sections of Christian transsexual culture the claim is made that an individual's true gender is determined by that person's mind and heart, and that only the persons concerned can say what their true gender is.[38]

The challenge is all the more intense when it is understood that in queer theory sexual identities are specifically understood as a function of representations. If I understand this theory correctly, it assumes that representations pre-exist and define, as well as complicate and disrupt sexual identities. Normative heterosexuality is seen as neither transcultural nor ahistorical. When boundaries are blurred to the point of invisibility, important questions around gendered identity surface immediately. Given the nexus with political, cultural, and social realities how are we to understand gender ethos and practice? Is there a mimetic dimension at work here, such that gender roles, far from expressing core identity, point instead towards the illusory and the ephemeral? Could this be a justification for both commitment and vocational fragility today? Given the almost automatic nature of gender bias[39] why are we surprised that situational factors continue to disrupt, disconcert, and give rise to anxiety on the one hand, and to issues of superiority, subordination, or equality on the other? Why am I identifying such issues? The whole purpose of this reflection is to equip the spiritual practitioner for real participation in the world that God loves.

Spirituality, especially in its applied and practical formulations, needs to enter into a critical dialogue with these new sources of information about human sexuality, gender, and identity. Such dialogue will be of concern to many within the Churches. It needs to do this in ways that respect distinctive cultural and diverse theological-religious frames of reference with their specific sex-gender assumptions, expectations, and habits of mind.[40] All of this raises a series of significant themes relevant to theology. Let me list four:

- formulations of gender theory and their theological implications for best practice in spiritual guidance;
- the theological uses and abuses of gender difference;
- problems with gender categories;
- issues to do with naming and imaging the Divine.[41]

In the absence of reflection on these and related themes, how is the spiritual or pastoral practitioner to relate understandingly to Christians whose gender is indeterminate, disturbing, or other? Add to this the impact of the advertising media. Gender bias is alive and well in the entertainment media, not least in dumbed down sitcoms and the adult entertainment industry.

GENDER, THEOLOGY AND SPIRITUAL PRAXIS

I. Some General Considerations

Almost twenty years ago Don Browning developed a view of the relationship between theology and prevailing cultural realities. It is worth revisiting because it has something to say to the dialogue between spirituality and social culture. Browning writes of a variety of relations between Christian praxis and contemporary cultural praxis. According to Browning the relation can be a matter of *identity* (the two might be highly congruent), of *non-identity* (they might be vastly different and perhaps antagonistic), or of *analogy* (the two might be different, but have many overlapping resemblances). He recalls the hermeneutical nature of practical theology. He notes that theologians in such reflections are always dealing with a variety of more or less adequate, more or less controversial interpretations, which have praxis implications for Christian witness.[42]

Spiritual guidance is, after all, practised in pluralistic public situations. It is related to the work of other professionals who treat with the inner lives of people, with their own praxis and their own theory of their praxis, some of it similar, some of it less so. For example, social workers, counsellors, psychologists, psychiatrists and others involved in the healing arts all deal with the inner life, address grief and loss, help rationalise the problem of suffering, and even help prepare for death. If Browning is correct, spiritual mentors need to be clear on the distinctiveness of their practice. They also need to be able to position their forms of praxis in complementary relationship with other caring modalities.[43] More, spiritual guides need to be able to navigate their way through the tangled issues and realities of contemporary women and men. In order to do this they need a well-based spiritual theology to guide them. One of the consequences of postmodern culture is that the Christian narrative ought to be as valid as any other narrative available today, one that has no need to apologise for its existence. Philip Sheldrake has observed that while one aspect of the postmodern highlights fragmentation, from another point of view it supports the understanding that the world and God are beyond the human mind and 'opens the possibility of a return to wonder and worship at the heart of theology and spirituality.'[44]

From practical theology, applied spirituality and spiritual guidance theory can learn to ask serious questions about the core realities of context and presence. Taking my cue from Don Browning, I suggest that applied spirituality, like practical theology, must have some depiction of the present situation, some critical theory about the ideal situation, and some understanding of how to get there. It needs to understand the processes, energies, paradigms and technologies required to generate authentic development even if that progress remains fragmentary and incomplete.[45] Further, it also needs to understand the vectors that shape spiritual experience.[46] All of these give rise to serious questions, in particular questions about the world of narrative, the ability to stay with deep, cognitive metaphor, the ability to engage a person or group's operative images of the Divine.[47] The dominant worldview has tremendous power to influence the way we think on a host of theological and philosophical issues. It is the challenge of theology to enter critical dialogue with the dominant worldview so that the gospel can cross the surging tides of time without being swept aside.[48] That said, it is important to recall that postmodernism is suspicious of the very desirability of conceptual schemes.[49] The modern era shows major signs of collapse, disintegration, and terminal decline. These are conditions that give rise to desperate, even dangerous endeavours to preserve and maintain previous stabilities and sensibilities.[50]

It is against such a background that a theologian, particularly one whose focus is in applied spirituality and spiritual guidance theory, reflects on human experience in relation to God. However, as Kathryn Tanner has written, 'such a focus for discussing human life also marks the theologian's humility, signalling the limits of the theological enterprise and the dependence of the theologian upon other forms of inquiry and other contexts of investigation.'[51] For spiritual theology what is of core concern is the relationship between people and a gift-bearing God in real historical situations. The human sciences inform us about people. The theologian 'takes up all that the sciences teach about human qualities and capacities in order to consider the manner and extent to which they may hinder or help human beings to fulfil their vocation of community and fellowship in relation to God.'[52] For the Christian, people are rooted in the meanings of the *imago Dei*.[53]

According to Tanner, there is something to a theological account of humanity even apart from its fleshing out by way of other modes of investigation.[54] When incorporated in a theological commentary, the conclusions of other disciplines at least undergo transposition into a religious key.[55] Tanner concludes that theology, 'on the basis of its understanding of God, proclaims the objective value of God's creatures, a value that must, therefore, be respected in the relations human beings establish with one another and with other kinds of beings in the world.'[56] The implications for applied spirituality and spiritual guidance theory are not far to seek.

Writing in *Cross Currents*, Douglas Hall offers an interesting vision of the nature of theology.[57] He describes it as an intellectual-spiritual activity that helps the Church to live creatively and faithfully between its worldly situation and its own particular sources of wisdom and hope. Metaphorically, this means living between context and text. That is to say, theology helps the Church discover 'gospel.' So, for example, in a social context where people are victims of poverty and political oppression, 'gospel' would certainly have something to do with economic, political and other forms of liberation. But it would also have something to do with the gendered subject living under such conditions. From a theological point of view, spiritual guidance practice must learn to bring the liberating gospel into places where it presently seems self-consciously out of place. This means recalling that the inter-locking systems of race, sexual orientation, social class, ecology, and gender not only shape everybody's experience, but also influence the desire for transformation. The sociology of knowledge cannot be ignored if spiritual practice is to be valid in a world where knowledge itself is conceived to be a form of power.

II.   The *Imago Dei* and Eschatology

I want to outline two theological responses to the complex challenges raised by contemporary views on sexuality, the body and gender. I will do this by drawing attention to the work of two contemporary theologians. According to Mary McClintock Fulkerson,[58] the intersection of secular and feminist theological thought, which she describes as social change practices, is in the gendered subject.[59] Her reflection on post-structuralism is instructive. She understands that by contesting constructionism it removes the notion of subjects altogether. In effect, post-structuralism generates an alternative account of difference grounded in a different understanding of language. Difference is the silence between words, the unsaid that makes meaning possible. Discourse always hides an Other. The net result of this is that the unique subject disappears in a world of silences and the inbetween. Oppression emerges as this Other is subjected to a normativity that does not apply. Otherness in this sense is experienced as a threat to the reigning normativity and by destabilising it faces us with mystery. The challenge is always that of uncovering what has been left unsaid, left outside, especially when we introduce the givenness of female and male sexed bodies. What Fulkerson learns from her post-structural reflection is that identity depends on a position within a system of differences.[60]

Fulkerson asserts 'the Christian belief that all are created *imago Dei*.'[61] This doctrine is central to theological thinking about the human person. The reference is to an original authentic human nature displayed in Jesus Christ that makes the human person capable of a relationship to God and affirms the goodness of finite life. In Fulkerson's view, 'by definition, to be creaturely is to be worthy of regard.'[62] 'As a naming of subjects of God's saving care, the *imago Dei* entails no essential definition of the subject, characterised only by finitude and God-dependence.'[63] This requires a growing capacity to recognise the silenced and the refused.[64] In this way forces of oppression may be recognised and resisted and individual and social change supported. Narrative – the hearing of stories rather than explanations – is the door because it aids the identifying of what is not being seen in a particular form of discourse. This involves recognising the limits of humanist and other paradigms. In the *imago Dei* the key has to do with the experiences of finitude and dependence, not sexuality, not gender.[65] Jesus on the Cross crosses out our partisan pre-understandings of God and ourselves.

Sarah Coakley offers a second helpful reflection. She writes that the obsessive interest in the body characteristic of Western culture in recent decades 'hides a profound eschatological longing; only a *theological* vision of a particular sort … can satisfy it.'[66] She discovers clues to that vision in the writings of Gregory of Nyssa and his eschatological goal, and finds interesting echoes of this eschatological longing in the influential work of Judith Butler. She claims that Butler's 'thematisations of desire, of gender fluidity, and subversive personal agency all echo older theistically-oriented traditions of transformation within and beyond the "body" of this mortal life.'[67] Coakley argues that Butler's theory 'has marks of a body longing for transformation into the divine.'[68] The eschatology that Coakley has in mind begins in the present with transformative practices whose final goal is in the future. It creates the future precisely by enacting its possibilities. According to Coakley, Gregory of Nyssa's gender theories do not claim to obliterate the gender binaries that remain culturally normative; he seeks to find a transformative way through them by redirecting *eros* towards the divine.

In Gregory's view the body is labile and changing. This involves a change that eventually reaches beyond this life into the next. It represents a continuum, an ongoing process of transformation into a perfection that is never arriving. This is a theology of anticipation, a leaning towards the future, an opening to it in the not yet. It involves openness to gender fluidity and volition on the one hand, and binary reversals on the other. For spiritual guidance theory this is the salient point. Such eschatological motility gives mortal flesh a final significance, a mysterious completion in a movement empowered by the Divine.[69] These ideas are not foreign to mystical literature. Spiritual guidance practitioners are sometimes privileged to accompany individuals whose contemplative experiences are characterised by the reality of such experiential reversals of normative gender assumptions. The most obvious example is in the area of nuptial or love mysticism where normal gender identities are eventually thrown into experiential reversal.[70]

An interesting example is in the case of a man struggling with the experience of being a *bride* of Christ, an experience that subverts his normative gender expectations and assumptions. Entry into such an experience is made possible to the extent that the individual achieves degrees of identity and gender fluidity that transcend egoic boundaries. A wide range of interweaving themes distinguishes this dimension of mystical and contemplative experience. These include *eros*, the vagaries of romantic attachments, love, desire, *agape*, invitation, intimacy, intensity, disturbance, resistance, and becoming to name just the most obvious. The call is towards unitary consciousness in a graced search for and encounter with the Beloved. This lures the individual beyond egoic possession or erotic defence into the freedom of *agape* where all distinctions and assumptions fall away precisely because it unfolds in a unitary state.[71] Unitive experience challenges all division.

Reflective Practice and Applied Spirituality
Applied spirituality must be able to address the whole spectrum of behavioural, social, and structural transformation. It is not sufficient for it to contribute only at the level of an interior spectrum of attitudes, beliefs, and espoused values.[72] The gendered subject, especially when that subject is silenced, marginalised or made into the invisible other, makes the need for an all-encompassing understanding of spiritual transformation imperative.[73] There is another point to be made here. It is the very nature of spiritual praxis to take the theme of Divine pedagogy seriously into account. In spiritual praxis the divine initiative is understood to be the ground, the thrust, and the horizon of contemporary spiritual theories of interpretation and response. The absence of this grounding principle leads inevitably to theoretical and interpretative distortion. This calls for a much more radical trust in God's self-disclosure than in the sovereignty of method. It calls for a more original and foundational commitment to concrete, existential-social-historical-contextual action that anticipates God's Domain. It calls for a more radical contemplative engagement in God's work of ongoing saving-healing-liberation and creation.[74]

Spiritual praxis needs to be informed by both local and global levels of research and analysis. At the same time, it needs to more fully comprehend the powerful influence of biblical and contemplative-mystical narratives. They have a potential for motivating spiritual and ethical action even in real-life postmodern contexts. Yet as Alan Jacobs has recently pointed out, the danger with certain approaches to narrative theology, for example, is precisely the neglect of the narrative dimension of individual Christian lives in favour of more communal narratives. No healthy, committed, and mature Christian is simply a generic Church member.[75] Spiritual guidance practitioners are challenged to hold both of these aspects together in a creative, transforming tension. Where systemic issues become more clearly involved, greater clarity is required in the spiritual praxis. This is primarily a reference to a quality and depth of reflective awareness, one that tends towards a more personal and existential appropriation of faith. In this context praxis, grounded in the graced love of the faith community, is itself understood to be the ground or cornerstone of theory, particularly since no theory in itself is ever innocent. Spiritual praxis may be compared to a dance of transformation. In this dance many horizons fuse and meet.[76] They interweave, inform, and lean towards liberating, transfiguring potentials. These are grounded in divine initiative and flower in response to the in-filling Spirit. In the postmodern context such transformation is important if revelation, grace, and genuine faith are to avoid distorting, reductive, or obscuring identifications with purely secular anthropologies and praxis.

Applied spirituality and spiritual guidance theory have an obvious cognate relationship with both pastoral and practical theology. While practical theology was developing, biblical studies experienced the challenge of modernity in terms of historical-critical approaches to scripture. In its turn, pastoral theology experienced it in terms of engagement with psychology, particularly clinical psychology, and the related human sciences. It is important that spiritual guidance practitioners continue to recognise the limits of the therapeutic paradigm even if this is not fully appreciated and recognised in other areas of spirituality. In recent years, for example, pastoral therapy has acquired the status of a clinical profession. It is vitally important that spiritual practice does not follow this path. The clinical approach, for all of the advances of transpersonal psychology,[77] is not well placed to deal with the issues that derive from the graced action of the divine Spirit. Don Browning drew attention to this problem when he wrote his study of religious thought and the psychologies fifteen years ago.[78] It is, of course, important that understandings of the intersecting of theological paradigms and social contexts take place in ways informed by both the social sciences and public policy. But it is equally important that spiritual guidance practice shifts to a clear focus on generativity and care against the background of a more informed cultural, social and religious context. In terms of the gendered subject, the 'living human web' suggests itself as the appropriate object for investigation, interpretation and transformation in spiritual guidance practice.[79]

Spiritual praxis also needs to be alert to media driven consumerist and leisure tendencies in contemporary spirituality. The problem with such approaches is that they continue to express mainstream normative thinking. The honest spiritual guidance practitioner will not collude with such practices. Subordinate individuals or groups in society already intimately know the realities of oppression, while the mainstream, given the predictable nature of mainstream psychology, continues to act in marginalising ways. The solution lies in a more humble approach to honest research and presence in applied spirituality.

Reflective practitioners in spiritual guidance are challenged to face such issues with open awareness and ethical humility. Of particular importance here is the recognition on the part of men that they are most likely unable, at least initially, to really hear women's stories. I refer here in particular to the sources of women's anger, to the painful depths of experiences of marginalisation, incest and rape, and to experiences of oppressive cultural or ecclesial stereotypes that so often define women's existence. Practitioners of spiritual guidance who cannot sit humbly, accurately, and contemplatively with these and related experiences need to question their personal commitment to growth and development. The self-respect of marginalised bearers of the *imago Dei* needs reverential contemplative holding. Spiritual practitioners need to recognise that in the uniqueness of individual lives knowledge is seldom universal or uniform. Most of the time truth remains contextual and tentative.

Such factors render the reflective practitioner more vulnerable to uncertain spaces where handy or favourite texts or the usually helpful answers seem irrelevant or oppressive. The spiritual practitioner who does not notice the influence of mainstream assumptions is blinded to what gender studies, feminist studies, black studies, and the studies of other marginalised groups in society all verify. The underprivileged, the marginalised, the outcast, and the silenced are bearers of real knowledge of real worlds. They confront practitioners with a range of counter-narratives: stories of marginalisation, brokenness stories, stories of struggle and survival, victim stories, stories of prejudice and exclusion. Such narratives stand against mainstream consensual reality and challenge its marginalising power. They open up hazardous spaces full of pointers to unrecognised or obscured or disturbing Spirit activity for those locked into mainstream perceptual systems. The challenge for spiritual practitioners – and others in the pastoral world – is this: if knowledge represents power, then power must be turned over to the silenced, to those rendered invisible as real people with genuine stories, bearers of the *imago Dei*. It is only then that the truly profound meaning of silence, of truly genuine contemplative listening, of the turn to the apophatic, will have its deepest impact on the spiritual practitioner alert to the call.[80]

The lesson is this: reflective practitioners must learn to hear the still small voice of what has been silenced or marginalised, what disrupts comfortable mainstream visions, precisely because these dimensions of life are worthy of Divine respect. This is something that spiritual and pastoral practitioners tend to know at an intellectual level. Dealing with it and articulating it in quite this way will be for many a new and challenging experience. It is for this reason that spiritual practitioners must eschew simplistic stances in favour of what ethnographers call *thick descriptions* of the realities they encounter.[81] This is made possible by contemplative humility and the beginner's mind. Spiritual practitioners have an opportunity to stand between the academy, the Church, and society, and through their contacts with real people in real locations, come to an awareness of the limits of academic exercises, and the limits of knowledge cut off from living contexts. It is for this reason that spiritual praxis, especially in life contexts that experience a blurring or severing of the relationship between religion and spirituality, challenges spiritual education to attend to its foundations.[82]

It is worth repeating that reflective spiritual practice names a quintessentially contemplative mode of relating that, as Thomas Merton has written, has no 'forgone conclusions'. Instead, it respects nature and respects the Holy Spirit.[83] The practitioner takes time for silent listening, which is often needed, and avoids getting caught up in activity that betrays the affect-laden, saviour-complexed impulse to try to fix things. The practitioner does tutor when that would be helpful. The practitioner quietly considers the other's story and need and helps to clarify it, attending to the Spirit, discerning the action of the Divine. The art of spiritual guidance calls for an inner dialogue with the Spirit of God at the same time that one is in dialogue with another human being. It focuses on the here and now, on a person's present life. It tracks the signs of God's presence in that life as the person tends towards the future, unfolding life to the full in a spiralling curve of ever deepening transformation. As Philip Sheldrake observes, spirituality points to another way of knowing and learning that is best understood as contemplative relationship where every attempt to speak of the Divine challenges the speaker to live spiritually.[84]

Concluding Reflections[85]

It is important to reiterate that the spiritual guidance practitioner working in postmodern contexts needs the human maturity, humility and contemplative wisdom to hear provocative insights, stories, counter-narratives, and experiences concerning a whole range of gender-oriented issues. Unfortunately, commonly held views of femininity and masculinity are more likely to oppress women. However, intra-gender oppression as well as inter-gender oppression is a statistical reality. There is a wealth of research available on this and related issues. There are more than simple stereotyping issues to be faced here. The constructs of masculinity and femininity are already at work at home and in school, as well as in society as a whole. They continually influence and challenge the work of spiritual guidance practitioners. Front-line practitioners, busily involved in pastoral care and retreat work which may not give them much time in which to come to know those they assist, represent the context in which stereotypical gender assumptions and images are most likely to be encountered and enacted. This means that the value base espoused by practitioners at this level is crucial. So also are retreatants' experiences in gender contexts in Church, family and society at large. Practitioners must clearly note the role of gender as a classification system in both socio-cultural and religious contexts. Such experiences represent a significant set of ideas, images and influences that need to be understood and taken into serious consideration.

The professional and ethical implications of experiential narratives give rise to serious questions not only to do with the influence of gendered assumptions on men and women's spiritual awareness, but also to do with the related questions of identity politics, identity selectivity, and identity relativism. How do social constructs and locations influence my own sense and experience of gender and its cognate categories? In the face of fiercely enforced social categories, as a man can I ask whether I truly want my unquestioned gender biases and assumptions to be surfaced and my status and privilege as an educated white male questioned?[86] In such a situation the claim of neutrality readily becomes just another cognitive trick intended to protect the very factors being challenged.

People's attitudes and perspectives, their stories and the accompanying sets of experiences, oppressions, and indeed, body knowledges are significant. They face us not only with crucial narrative or counter-narrative resources, but also with the implications of social gradients in relationships across the whole spectrum of personal, social, cultural and religious privilege up to and including abusive betrayals of trust.[87] It is worth recalling here that research has begun to show just how pervasive and damaging spiritual abuse is in people's lives. It takes from people the ability to make sense of the ultimate questions and find meaning in their lives. There is also the crosscut of issues grounded in understandings of class, ethnicity and formative religious backgrounds. All of these factors challenge practitioners to hold diversity and difference in contemplative awareness. This in turn raises the issue of a practitioner's personal growth and development and makes the ethical necessity of qualified supervision self-evident.

The presence of power issues in gender contexts is now an established position. Yet understandings are always partial, knowledge incomplete, and practice itself draws on traditions, theories and personal experience. Carol Gilligan's work is a case in point. It identifies the manner in which even research is judged in gender contexts.[88] Already in 1988, the historian J. Wallach Scott claimed that gender bias represented a fundamental way of signifying power.[89] Unconscious privilege, and the implied power gradient that tends to be covertly present, remains a primary source of inter-gender misunderstanding and oppression. The whole question of archetypal and collective influences active at the level of the psyche itself also needs to be considered. The work of Jean Shinoda Bolen[90] and Polly Young-Eisendrath[91] is significant in this context. Appropriate hermeneutical questions must be asked about the historical gender contexts of the originators of theories, traditions, practices and policies in both spirituality and culture if we are to understand the tensions that have become increasingly evident in postmodern contexts.

Challenging stereotypes at the theoretical level is not enough. The complex sets of issues that intersect in the sexuality-gender-identity triad have to be brought to the level of practical action if they are ever to inform best practice. This will more predictably happen when simplistic assumptions and images of God and Church, grace and charism, discipleship and discernment, masculinity and femininity, which ignore complexities or complications, are challenged by more complex interactions and discourses that look critically at the theological, historical or related factors that support them. Complex gender identity issues cannot be ignored if fully-rounded, authentic transformation is to result. The implications for best practice and training in spiritual guidance are profound. The lived experience of the sexuality-gender-identity triad and its cognate themes will remain a challenge. It will require attentive reflection and investigation if the spiritual practitioner is to deal wisely with the disruptions and opportunities postmodern fluidity and fragmentation generate in the lives of women and men who stand before God in Church and world.

Notes

1   'Postmodern' names the point of view in philosophy and culture that there is no independent reality, no metanarratives, no objective truth, where everything is fragmentary, superficial, individualistic and subjectivistic, and no unified subject.

2   P. Sheldrake, *Spaces for the Sacred,* (London: SCM Press, 2001) 30.

3   See D. Quinn (2004) 'Prelate Outlines Vision for Future of Church' in *Irish Independent* Tuesday, 10 February, p. 4. Quinn reports on Dr Diarmuid Martin's comments at a recent seminar on parish renewal at All Hallows College, Dublin. The Archbishop addressed the issue of women's presence in offices at all levels of the Church. In the course of his presentation he drew attention to the problem of a closed, blocked clerical system and the need to address male prejudices and fears.

4   This calls for an awareness of the variety of cultural forms through which the *male-female* binary is understood, and the ways in which the binary *sex-gender* is both constructed and used. Such an understanding is particularly significant to comprehending how women and men's social identity is constructed. While the total disconnection of concepts of *masculinity* and *femininity* from biological differences is untenable, the influence of cultural and socialisation dynamics cannot be ignored. This is especially so in terms of the systems of ideas around which theories of sexual identity and difference are themselves built. See, for example, J. Fulcher & J. Scott, *Sociology,* (Oxford: OUP, 1999) 139-147, 179-185, 191-196, 249-253, 294-301 for an overview of these themes.

5   E. Liebert, *Changing Life Patterns. Adult Development in Spiritual Direction,* (St Louis: Chalice Press, 2000) 7.

6   K. Leech, *Spirituality and Pastoral Care* (London: Sheldon Press, 1986), 48.

7   P. Sheldrake, op.cit., 90.

8   It is important to note that the word *spirituality* is a moving concept in English usage, one that defies simple definition. See, for example, L.L. LaPierre, 'A Model

for Describing Spirituality' in K.J. Collins, ed., *Exploring Christian Spirituality: An Ecumenical Reader* (Grand Rapids MI: Baker Books, 2000) 74-82.

9   Radical relativism is a serious concern for those involved in spirituality and theology because it makes space only for fictions, points of view, opinions, feelings and impressions. For an overview of the issues, opportunities and challenges of postmodernity see, for example, R.C. Greer, *Mapping Postmodernism. A Survey of Christian Options* (Downers Grove IL: Intervarsity Press, 2003).

10   This is the term coined by Wittgenstein to describe the way in which language follows paradigmatic rules according to which truth is only self-evident within the parameters of a given paradigm.

11   See D.S. Browning, 'Practical Theology and Political Theology' in *Theology Today* 42 1 (April, 1985), 15-33.

12   *Parataxic distortion* names the way in which distortion predictably enters human relationships as a consequence of largely unrecognised patterns of relational reaction. It names a predetermined way of relating to individuals with certain characteristics and supports prejudices grounded in earlier relational experiences and the projections and paranoia often associated with them.

13   See S. Coakley, *Powers and Submissions: Spirituality, Philosophy and Gender,* (Oxford: Blackwell, 2002).

14   L. Layton, 'Cultural Hierarchies, Splitting, and the Heterosexist Unconscious' in S.Fairfield, L.Layton, & C. Stack, eds., *Bringing the Plague: Toward a Postmodern Psychoanalysis,* (New York: Other Press, 2002) 195-223.

15   Coakley, op.cit. p. xiii.

16   See, for example, M. Althaus-Reid, *Indecent Theology: Theological Perversions in Sex, Gender and Politics*, (London: Routledge, 2000).

17   S. Connor, *Postmodernist Culture: An Introduction to Theories of the Contemporary* (Oxford: Blackwell, 1989) 229.

18   Consider emotional, cognitive, imagistic, spiritual, and theological literacy to name but a few.

19   Consider the complex interweaving of historical, political, social, ideological, institutional, sexual, gender, and psychological influences to name just the most obvious.

20   Cognition has to do with the mental processes of knowing, such as awareness, perception, reasoning, intuition and judgment.

21   P. Young-Eisendrath, *Gender and Desire: Uncursing Pandora* (College Station: Texas A&M University Press, 1997) 26-58.

22   Quoted in Coakley, op.cit. p. 158.

23   See ibid. p. 159.

24   H. Ferguson, *Modernity and Subjectivity: Body, Soul, Spirit* (Charlottsville & London: University Press of Virginia, 2000) 20-79, note p. 65.

25   See J. Culler, *Literary Theory: A Very Short Introduction* (Oxford & New York: OUP, 1997) 99-100.

26   J. Norton, 'Bodies that Don't Matter: the Discursive Effacement of Sexual Difference' in *Women and Language* 20/1 (1997) at 24ff.

27   S. Fairfield, 'In Our Consciousness, In Our conscience, In Our Backyard' in Fairfield et al, op.cit., (2002) 113-127 at 119.

28   See A-M Smith, *Julia Kristeva: Speaking the Unspeakable,* (London: Pluto Press, 1998) 52-53.

29   See M. D. Kirtley & J. B. Weaver, 'Exploring the Impact of Gender Role Self-Perception on Communication Style' in *Women's Studies in Communication* 22/2 (1999) at 190.

30   S. White, 'As the World Turns: Ontology and Politics in Judith Butler' in *Polity* 30/2 (1999) at 155ff.

31   See R. Eisler, *Sacred Pleasure: Sex, Myth, and the Politics of the Body* (New York: HarperSanFrancisco, 1996) 244-264.

32   See B. Krais, 'Gender and Symbolic Violence: Female Oppression in the light of Pierre Bourdieu's Theory of Social Practice' in C.E. LiPuma Calhoun & M. Postone (Eds.), *Bourdieu: Critical Perspectives* (Cambridge: Polity Press, 1993) 156-177 at 170.

33   M. Foucault, *The History of Sexuality: Volume 1* (R. Hurley, Trans.). (New York: Vintage, 1978), 11.

34   P. Bourdieu, *The Field of Cultural Production*. (P.R. Nice, Trans.) (Cambridge: Polity, 1993) 236.

35   Op. cit., pp. 201-212.

36   See Fulcher & Scott, op.cit. pp. 66-67.

37   See W. Throckmorton, 'Attempts to Modify Sexual Orientation: A Review of Outcome Literature and Ethical Issues' in *Journal of Mental Health Counseling* 20 (October, 1998) 283-304.

38   Log on to www.whosoever.org.

39   N. Ambady & J.A. Richeson, 'Who's in Charge? Effects of Situational Roles on Automatic Gender Bias' in *Sex Roles: A Journal of Research* (2001) 493ff.

40   See J. Mezirow, 'Learning to Think like an Adult' in J. Mezirow and Associates, *Learning as Transformation. Critical Perspectives on a Theory in Progress* (San Francisco: Jossey-Bass, 2000) 3-33, in particular 16-24.

41   See, for example, S. Frank Parsons, ed., *The Cambridge Companion to Feminist Theology* (Cambridge: CUP, 2002).

42   Browning, op.cit. See in particular the discussion on p. 18.

43   Ibid.

44   P. Sheldrake, *Spirituality and Theology: Christian Living and the Doctrine of God* (London: DLT, 1998) 27.

45   See Browning, op.cit. p. 20.

46   See D.L. Gelpi SJ, *Experiencing God: A Theology of Human Emergence* (New York/Ramsey/Toronto: Paulist Press, 1978) 75-97.

47   Operative images and beliefs are contrasted with espoused images and beliefs because they are the ones that come into operation in life contexts.

48   L. I. Sweet, 'Straddling Modernism and Postmodernism' in *Theology Today* 47/2 (July 1990) 159-164, at 162.

49   Ibid., p. 163.

50   Ibid., p. 164.

51   K. Tanner, 'The Difference Theological Anthropology Makes' in *Theology Today* 50/4 (January, 1994) 567-579 at 567.

52   Ibid., p. 574.

53   Ibid., pp. 572-573.

54   Ibid., p. 577.

55   Ibid., p. 578.

56   Ibid., p. 579.

57   D. J. Hall (2003). 'What Is Theology?', in *Cross Currents*, 53 (Summer, 2002), at 171ff.

58   M. McClintock Fulkerson, 'Contesting the Gendered Subject: A Feminist Account of the Imago Dei' in R.S. Chopp & S. Greeve Daveney, *Horizons in Feminist Theology: Identity, Tradition, and Norms*, (Minneapolis: Fortress Press, 1997) 95-115.

59   Ibid., p. 99.

60   Ibid., pp. 103-107.

61   Ibid., p. 107.

62   Ibid., pp. 107-108.

63   Ibid., p. 108.

64   See Ibid., pp. 108-111.

65   Ibid., pp. 111-115.

66   Coakley op.cit. p. 153, her emphasis.

67   Ibid., p. 157.

68   Ibid.

69   Ibid., pp.157-167.

70   In the 12th century a new type of mysticism in which love was the central theme emerged. The most extensive description of this mysticism was given by Jean de Fécoup.

71   See, for example, J.K. Ruffing, *Spiritual Direction: Beyond the Beginnings* (London: St Paul's Publishing 2000) particularly 95-123. See also G. May, *Will and Spirit: A Contemplative Psychology*, (New York: HarperCollins, 1982). This classic text should be required reading for the serious spiritual practitioner.

72   See M. Downey, *Understanding Christian Spirituality* (New York/Mahwah: Paulist Press, 1997).

73   See W.E. Conn, *The Desiring Self. Rooting Pastoral Counselling and Spiritual Direction in Self-Transcendence* (New York/Mahwah: Paulist Press, 1998).

74   See, for example, J. W. Fowler, 'Practical Theology and Theological Education: Some Models and Questions' in *Theology Today* 42/ (April, 1985) 43-58.

75   A. Jacobs, 'What Narrative Theology Forgot' in *First Things* 135(August/September 2003) 25-30.

76   See T. St. James O'Connor, *Clinical Pastoral Supervision and the Theology of Charles Gerkin* (Waterloo Ontario: Wilfrid Laurier University Press, 1998).

77   See for example, J.N. Ferrer, *Revisioning Transpersonal Theory: A Participatory Vision of Human Spirituality* (Albany: State University of New York Press, 2002); and M. Washburn, *Embodied Spirituality in a Sacred World*, (Albany: State University of New York Press, 2003).

78   See D.S. Browning, *Religious Thought and the Modern Psychologies* (Philadelphia: Fortress Press, 1987).

79   See B. J. Miller-Mclemore, 'The Human Web: Reflections on the State of Pastoral Theology' in *The Christian Century* 110/11 (April, 1993) 366ff.

80   See A. Hollywood, *Sensible Ecstasy: Mysticism, Sexual Difference, and the Demand of History* (Chicago & London: The University of Chicago Press, 2002) 96-99.

81   The term is attributed to Clifford Geertz. See his 'Thick Description: Toward an Interpretative Theory of Culture' in *The Interpretation of Cultures*, (New York: Basic Books, 1973). *Thick descriptions* emerge as practitioners tell stories, offer

a range of metaphorical redescriptions, ethnographies both emic and etic, fairy tales, mythologies, religious texts and biographies and histories as they explore the relationship between contingencies and regularities in the precarious spaces of people's lives. See, for example, J. Law, *Organizing Modernity,* (Oxford: Blackwell, 1994), 12-18.

82   Miller-McLemore, op. cit.

83   See E.G. Stout & P.M. Pearson, eds., 'Thomas Merton on Spiritual Direction' in *Presence 9/3* (October, 2003) 39-43, at 41.

84   Sheldrake, *Spirituality and Theology,* op. cit., 30-32.

85   I owe a debt of gratitude to Joan Orme's work, which triggered these reflections. See J. Orme, *Gender and Community Care. Social Work and Social Care Perspectives* (Basingstoke & New York: Palgrave, 2001).

86   These and related factors hide power issues. See Adolf Guggenbuhl-Craig's classic text *Power in the Helping Professions*, (Dallas: Spring Publications, tenth printing, 1990). The text was originally published in 1971.

87   See R. Radford Reuther, ed., *Gender, Ethnicity, and Religion. Views from the Other Side* (Minneapolis: Fortress Press, 2002).

88   See in particular C. Gilligan, *In A Different Voice* (London: Harvard University Press, 1993).

89   J. Wallach Scott, *Gender and the Politics of History*, (Columbia University Press, 1988), 43.

90   J. Shinoda Bolen, *Goddesses in Everywoman: A New Psychology of Women.* (San Francisco: Harper & Row, 1984); *Gods in Everyman: A New Psychology of Men's Lives and Loves* (San Francisco: Harper & Row, 1984).

91   P. Young-Eisendrath, *You're Not What I Expected: Love After the Romance Has Ended* (New York: Fromm International Paperback, 1997).

THE HUMAN SPIRIT AND THE OPTION FOR THE ECONOMICALLY POOR

MICHAEL O'SULLIVAN SJ

The great majority of the world's people are economically poor. For example, 1.3 billion people in a world of six billion people live on less than $1 dollar a day; about 840 million people are malnourished; 100 million people are homeless; 2.6 billion people have no access to sanitation; two billion people have no electricity; about one in five of the world's children of primary school age is out of school; and in New York City, 52 per cent of children are born into poverty.[1] Not only does poverty affect the quality of people's lives, it also robs them unjustly and prematurely of quantitative lifetime.[2] For example, while life expectancy at birth in Ireland is 76.6 years, the corresponding figure for Sierra Leone, one of the economically poorest countries in the world, is 38.9 years.[3] This disturbing and outrageous situation calls for a preferential option for the poor. The foundation to justify such an option can be found in the interiority of the human spirit. People can find this foundation in themselves to be religious as well as ethical, and the religious foundation can enter a Christian mode.[4] What follows explains this position.

The Transcendental Spirit of Desire
In order for a situation like global economic poverty to make an impact on people in a way that will move them to want to know and do something about it, the situation will have to be accessible to human consciousness. Self-attention discloses that such accessibility is possible because a human person exists with a mysterious and foundational

spirit of desire in his or her interiority that makes him or her want to know things as they are, why they are that way, and to make decisions in accordance with such knowledge for the sake of positive transformation in the world. This spirit is a transcendental spirit because it is a priori, unrestricted, and comprehensive. It is a priori because it exists in the person before the person knows that it does. It is not a product of knowledge and decision, but the always prior and empowering condition for the possibility of knowledge and decision, including knowledge about itself. It is unrestricted because its dynamism is structured by inner functioning anticipations of concrete beauty, intelligibility, truth, goodness and love, which drive it forward beyond what would restrict it from reaching the beauty, intelligibility, truth, goodness and love corresponding to a particular situation. This also means that this exigent spirit has an inbuilt criterion of authenticity to guide a person's knowing and choosing. It is comprehensive because it seeks, not just the beauty, intelligibility, truth, goodness and love concerning particular situations, but the fullness of the mysterious unknown. Because of this transcendental character the human spirit can be called 'the passionateness of being' in human interiority.[5]

This spirit of desire, or passionateness of being, in human consciousness functions, not only with anticipations of beauty, intelligibility, truth, goodness and love, but also through four basic operations of human consciousness, namely, experiencing, understanding, judging and deciding, and on four corresponding levels of consciousness, namely, experience, understanding, judgement and decision. The operations and levels have an altruistic character. Each operation and level functions in the light of what the other operations and levels need to empower the transcendental spirit in the human person to reach the beauty, truth, goodness, and love it desires in a given instance. Each operation and level, in other words, makes an autonomous, but related, contribution under the impact of the person's transcendental desire to what is a unified and shared task.

The Contraries: The Modes of Discovery and Belief

This dynamic altruistic activity of desire-filled consciousness in human subjectivity is discovered by the self-attentive person to function according to two modes of knowledge and decision. These two modes are those of discovery and belief.[6] In the mode of knowledge and decision through discovery, experiential consciousness in the human person attends to data and makes available to the person's intellectual consciousness, where questioning occurs, the relevant data it needs for interpretative understanding; intellectual consciousness raises questions about the supplied data and makes available to the critical consciousness in the person the insights and interpretations it needs to make a judgement concerning, not what is simply plausible, but what is actually or probably correct; and critical consciousness weighs up the offered interpretations and makes available to moral consciousness the reliable knowledge a person needs to make there a decision concerning what course of action to implement.[7]

In the contrary, but not contradictory, order of knowledge and decision through belief, the human person at the inner depth level in himself or herself of his or her transcendental desire begins with a decision in affectivity to trust, and on that basis proceeds to develop judgements concerning what is believable, an understanding of the meaning of the beliefs, and a way of communicating that understanding to transform the experience of those in the historical situation. Thus, while knowledge evokes a responsible love as the culmination of the process of knowing and choosing in the mode of discovery, a commitment to love originates knowledge in the mode of belief.

The Contradictories: The Modes of Authenticity and Inauthenticity
The contraries that are the two modes of knowing and decision in the human person are subject to the contradictories that are the modes of authenticity and inauthenticity.[8] In order for the human person to reach the truth that she or he desires at a transcendental depth level concerning a historical situation like global poverty, and to originate through decisions the goodness consistent with such truth, she or he must operate and combine the respective contraries according to the standard of authenticity. Such activity involves the person in a transcendental and historically contextualised praxis of authentic subjectivity.

Authentic Subjectivity and Social Transformation: The Modes of Praxis
Praxis means to think and theorise in and in relation to a context of transformation. The transcendental praxis of authenticity is a form of praxis because the person in such praxis thinks and theorises, not about, the situation of the economically poor, for example, but about the functioning of his or her own operations of consciousness thinking and theorising about that situation, and seeks to change such functioning when there is a conflict with the standard of authenticity. Such a conflict exists when a person discovers that his or her

experiencing, understanding, judging and deciding, are subject to ignorance, bias, fear, and denial, etc. The transcendental form of praxis, therefore, seeks to promote the transformative effect of authenticity in and in relation to these operations of consciousness in *the human person*. It seeks to promote the person to undergo a psychic, intellectual, moral and religious conversion of consciousness that is consistent with the authentic dynamism of its own consciousness. This means it seeks to promote the person to a standard of functioning in his or her own consciousness where the censor does not function repressively, but constructively, in terms of the images, symbols and psychic energies it releases, or does not release, and where the person is able to apprehend reality under the aesthetic aspect of the beautiful (psychic conversion); where it asks all the relevant questions about the unknown and does not settle for answers that do not do justice to what is being demanded by such questions (intellectual conversion); where it chooses what is to be done in accordance with the standard of value, or what is truly worthwhile, and not what is merely pleasing, pleasurable, convenient, comfortable, conventional or cowardly (moral conversion); and where it surrenders to the call to be in love in an unrestricted way with the mystery of goodness at the heart of life (religious conversion).[9]

Because these operations of consciousness in the person, and the conversions that fulfil their potential to function authentically in relation to the inbuilt anticipations of the operations for beauty, intelligibility, truth, goodness and love, are characteristic of the person as human, what one person discovers and decides through these converted operations is not merely subjective, but can be replicated and verified by others for themselves. In this way human persons learn that they share a normative method in consciousness that makes dialogue and cooperation between them in the direction of objectivity possible.

This transcendental praxis is, always, a contextualised praxis because of the situated character of the desire-filled human subject. As such it seeks to promote the transformative effect of authenticity within the human person in and in relation to *a historical situation*. It does this in the case of global economic poverty by promoting the human person to think and theorise about such poverty in a way that can lead to the development of meaning and value that can transform the situation of poverty into one that is instead truly good, beautiful and loving for people. Self-liberation in the praxis of authenticity promotes the human person to the self-transcending level of being an authentic and effective agent in the social praxis of transformation of lived meaning and value concerning such poverty. This self-liberation in the interest of social transformation reaches its peak in the state of being in love without reserve, which is what religious conversion as an event of consciousness means. In this state the human person is not content to do what is right and just, but is moved beyond these standards to do what is not required, because love does that to a person. It enables him or her to feel, be aware of, imagine and conceive higher possibilities in a situation, and moves him or her to act gratuitously. As a result it alters the probabilities of what is possible concerning the transformation of a situation like that of global economic poverty. This general religious conversion of consciousness becomes a conversion to the specific religious tradition of authentic Catholic meaning and value when God's love in Jesus Christ is identified as the source and term of desire filled consciousness. Then there is 'nothing in all creation that can separate us from the love of God in Christ Jesus our Lord' (Rom 8:38-39). On the foundation and in the horizon of such a specific religious conversion authentic Christian meaning and value become the standard of authenticity for the human spirit seeking genuine beauty, intelligibility, truth, goodness and love in and in relation to the global situation of economic poverty.

As a person, therefore, attends to the reality of global economic poverty from a perspective of self-attention to the character of authenticity of his or her foundational common human spirit, she or he finds in that spirit a foundation and horizon for people to know and do what is required of them if they are to transform the situation of poverty. Their discovery may lead them to choose the authentic Christian tradition as the foundation and horizon for such social transformation.

The Human Good and Global Poverty

A conversion to the authentic Christian tradition as the fulfilling ground of what the transcendental human spirit desires in the face of the challenge of global economic poverty is strengthened by a person's discovery that the dynamic structure of that spirit mediates a method that is conducive to a preferential option for the economic poor of the world. What follows clarifies this statement. Through continuing self-attention to his or her foundational human spirit a person can discover that people at the level of common human experience in themselves seek such human goods as food, shelter, clothing, relaxation, education, health and friendship. At the level of common human understanding they seek a way of organising the data that these particular goods desired in experience are. This means that they seek the good of social order. At the level of common human judgement they weigh up the claims of different understandings of social order concerning how best to organise the data of experience. They seek the system that actually has the highest probability of delivering in a recurrent way the particular goods desired. And at the level of common human decision they deliberate until they find the course of action that offers the highest probability of implementing their judgement effectively. All this occurs when they are functioning as they can, that is, authentically, and occurs in a deficient way otherwise.

Because these interrelated levels of experience, understanding, judgement and decision in a human person are common to all human persons, what is mediated by the interrelated operations of experiencing, understanding, judging, and deciding on the respective levels is a shared human good, so that in the measure in which people are tuned into the authenticity of their subjectivity and are committed to its implications they will be moved to cooperate in the construction of an objective common good.

The dynamism of desire for the truly human good in the context of global economic poverty mediates into consciousness the contradiction of authentic human wellbeing that is the contemporary global order. It also leads to the emergence of feelings that make it possible to apprehend the value in terms of which a judgement can be made concerning which social system proposed by understanding is preferable. This transcendental, or foundational, apprehension of value in feelings is facilitated by historical experiences and feelings that tune one into the pain of oppressed people and the beauty and goodness of their liberation. In this way the value of a system constituted by a preferential option for the economically poor emerges in consciousness, and a judgment is made that this indeed is the way to create a new global order. This judgement evokes a decision to make the apprehended and affirmed value of a preferential option for the poor a practical reality by working for 'globalisation from below.'[10]

Religious Conversion and Globalisation 'From Below'
At this level of felt-value-laden decision the person as a transcendental subject of activity emerges as an ethical subject. However, this subject is moved to religious conversion in the context of a decision to opt for

globalisation from below by the imperative from within his or her own being to ground his or her option in ultimate meaning and value. This transcendental drive to ultimate meaning and value as the foundation and horizon for ethical action makes the situated human person tune in even more deeply to the mysteriousness of his or her being and can open him or her to the historical religious meaning and value that Christian revelation offers as ultimate meaning and value, especially where such meaning and value is part of the cultural matrix.

Where such meaning and value are already constitutive of the person's life, it will lead the person to re-read them in the light of the new situation. In both cases the human person reads Christian revelation through the hermeneutical resonance of the praxis of authenticity of his or her own being as he or she seeks a relationship with Christianity that is expressive of a life of integrity.[11]

A re-reading of this kind recovers a reported central trajectory within scripture concerning a belief by others in a mystery of infinite beauty, truth, goodness, and love named God that calls people to a preferential option for the economically poor. This fundamental option is revealed in the liberating events of the Exodus,[12] the communion between this God and the people in the Covenant, the call of the Prophets to the people to remain faithful to their covenant with this God, the refusal of the remnant in exile to give up on their belief in this God's abiding fidelity to them, and the person and praxis of Jesus of Nazareth who declared that the Spirit of the Lord had sent him to bring good news to the poor and liberty to captives,[13] and whose resurrection affirmed, it was believed, his historical option of universal salvation through social liberation from below.[14] This reading of scripture is facilitated by the writings of theologians like Gustavo Gutierrez, a pioneer from Peru, of Liberation theology.

The person who is moved by the dynamism of his or her depth level of desire towards beauty, truth, goodness and love to undergo conversion to this mediated biblical God moves from knowledge and decision through discovery to knowledge and decision through belief. By doing so she or he recognises and accepts that the self-communicated God who is witnessed to by the Christian tradition is, not only the fulfilment of the 'desire-as-gift' orientation of his or her subjectivity, but also the source of that desire, so that the revealed outer self-communication in Jesus Christ ultimately explains and fulfils the dynamism of the inner gifted spirit.[15] This means that Christian revelation is not a transcendental deduction, something reducible to a merely human event, an achievement of human reason, but is instead an event of divinely initiated intersubjectivity.

The divine initiative in a Christian religious conversion is gratuitous, and the conversion is also dramatic because in its revelation of the gift of Jesus Christ it goes way beyond what might be expected. It is, also, however, in harmony with the intentional trajectory of the foundational desire of human subjectivity because such a desire and its trajectory are elements oriented to the gift of that divinely originated saving grace.

A person who lives a Christian religious conversion functions in interiority in a way that decides to trust what scripture offers is evidence concerning not just a report of what others have believed and thought, but the *reality* of who God is; to judge as believable that this God has entered the world as a universal saviour in Jesus Christ; to understand that this doctrine of salvation can be conceived to mean that God's universal saving love is available and made effective through a preferential option for the economically poor;[16] and to communicate such understanding to others by transformative lived practice. The situated human person who arrives at this point when faced with global economic poverty will promote the work of globalisation from below as central to Christian redemption on the foundation and in the horizon of the praxis of authenticity of his or her religiously converted transcendental human subjectivity to the authentic Christian tradition.

Behind the emergence, for some, of a Christian conversion that is bound up with the situation of the economically poor may be prophetic mystical experience that should not be regarded as reserved only for an elite.[17] Such experience may hve emerged in prayerful attention to the God of the Christian tradition in the context of a person dealing with key events in his or her life that need not have been concerned about the situation of global poverty. The experience can be explained by the inner activity in human subjectivity of the Spirit that is in the Trinity establishing in interaction with what is happening for the person at such times in his or her life a dynamic state of being in love with God as the foundation and horizon of how to live the first and only edition of the person's life. An experience I had thirty years ago will illustrate what I mean, and conclude this article.

The Role of Religious Experience: An Autobiographical Example
During 1973–74, the final year of my studies for a degree in social science at University College Dublin, I was struggling with my Jesuit vocation. Because of this struggle I sometimes found myself alone at

night, when my friends were sleeping or praying in the community oratory in Rathfarnham Castle.[18] On one of those nights, and quite unexpectedly, the scene of Jesus in Gethsemane appeared before me. It did so in a way that held me, and kept me focused. There seemed to be no effort on my part, as though everything that was happening was being shown to me, and in a way that was so vivid, real, and illuminating. The next thing I knew I was in tears, as the inner Jesus was revealed to me. I saw with stunning clarity his inside life of tremendous, courageous love. This, then, was the secret of his motivation. It was behind the stands he took. It kept him going. It meant he would not give up, even when vulnerable to great inner suffering and external danger. As this extraordinary courageous love took hold of me I felt myself strengthened to continue on in my vocation. I experienced God's answer to my own struggle at that time and to what my life could mean for the future. I was being called to remain a Jesuit in order to live the same kind of heroic love of Jesus. I, too, would suffer in the process, almost certainly, but God would see me through. God and I were in it together. I felt the intimacy of that connection and assurance. It was not clear to me then in what way precisely I would experience the call to be courageous like Jesus; I only knew that I had left myself open to receiving it and that it would come.

In the summer of 1975 I spent four weeks in what was then the Jesuit novitiate at Manresa House, Dublin praying and reflecting on the documents of the recently concluded 32nd General Congregation of the Jesuits.[19] At the end of that period I experienced a conversion to the newly articulated Jesuit mission to serve the faith that promotes justice as an absolute requirement. This conversion was due to the effect on me of my foundational commitment in love to the God I had met about eighteen months earlier in Rathfarnham interacting with the new prayerfully mediated meaning and value concerning how to be a Jesuit in the modern world from the Congregation. As a result of this conversion I have tried to live my Jesuit life since that time by taking clear and courageous stands in different ways and places on behalf of the economically poor, women, and people of other races.

These responses have sometimes resulted in forms and depths of suffering I had not expected. This suffering has dragged me down, and sometimes I have felt I could not go on. But then the experience in Rathfarnham oratory would come again and renew my spirit. Because of it, and other graces like deep friendships, the discovery of the positive difference I have made in the lives of some, and the inspiration of the goodness of some, I understand now more fully the redemptive character of the enlightening and empowering role of religious experience in the work of justice and love. Such religious experience of gifted initiative from the mystery that we call God, either through focused prayer experience or in interactive experience with people, which religious experience need not have been related to the situation of th economically poor, can subsequently make it possible for a person to develop, not only an option for those who are treated as though they are non-persons,[20] like the economically poor, and to conceive that option in relation to redemption in the love of Jesus Christ, but also a capacity to link up with others of a similar experience and to endure, like Jesus, in that option in the face of the inevitable pain and hardship that it brings. In this way I have learned from religious experience that gifted initiative from the mystery that we call God at a turning point in a person's life can become foundational in interiority for subsequent options of cooperative grace, such as giving a priority to the economically poor, in the first an only edition of the person's life.

Notes

1. These statistics appeared in a table by Paul Cullen in *The Irish Times* (December 31, 1999). The table was compiled from the following sources: UNDP, WHO, UNICWF, Dataquest, Forbes, the *Economist* and Transparency International.

2. Gustavo Gutierrez, a pioneer of Liberation Theology, makes this point frequently in his writings.

3. This figure is given in a table by Liam Reid, 'How Ireland compares to the poorest country in the world,' *Sunday Tribune* (August 25, 2002) 18. It is not differentiated according to gender.

4. Bernard Lonergan has articulated the dynamism and structure of the desire-filled transcendental human subject in his writings. See in particular *Insight, Method in Theology, Collection, Second Collection* and *A Third Collection.* The articulation, however, has to be read as an aid to, rather than as a substitute for, the activity of one's self-appropriation as a knower and doer. As Haughey says, '(Lonergan's) method is not *his* method but *our* method if we can see what goes into thinking our thoughts and making our choices.' See John C. Haughey, SJ, 'Responsibility for Human Rights: Contributions from Bernard Lonergan,' *Theological Studies* 63 (2002) 764-785 at 783.

5. 'Mission and the Spirit,' in *A Third Collection: Papers by Bernard J.F. Lonergan, SJ,* ed. Frederick E. Crowe, SJ (Mahwah, NJ: Paulist Press, 1985) 23-34 at 29.

6. See 'Natural Right and Historical Mindeness,' in *A Third Collection: Papers by Bernard J. F. Lonergan, SJ,* ed. Frederick E. Crowe, SJ (New York: Paulist Press, 1985), 180-81.

7. Note that knowledge is a compound reality of experience, understanding and judgment. It also involves belief, as the mode of knowledge through belief makes clear.

8 Robert Doran, SJ distinguishes contraries and contradictories as follows: 'Contraries are reconcilable in a higher synthesis, while contradictories exclude one another.' See his *Theology and the Dialectics of History* (Toronto, Buffalo and London: University of Toronto Press, 1990) 10.

9 Religious conversion is an event of consciousness before it is an event of conversion to a specific religious tradition. In the concrete, however, people tend to seek the symbolisation and institutionalisation of a religious conversion, which is to say that in the concrete such a conversion tends to occur with reference to a specific religious tradition.

10 Professor Robert Falk, Princeton University, has coined this phrase. Gustavo Gutierrez had spoken in the same way years earlier when he declared that Christian salvation had to be a salvation of integral liberation from below, that is, from the side of the economically poor, and of 'non-persons' in general. See, Gustavo Gutierrez, *The Power of the Poor in History*, (New York: Maryknoll, Orbis, 1983 (Spanish original, 1979) 22, and 169-221. Gutierrez has appealed to Dietrich Bonhoeffer as a support for this worldview. See *Power*, 203, and 230-33. .

11 Hermeneutics is the theory of interpretation.

12 See N. K. Gottwald's account of how to understand the faith and history of what came to be called Israel in his *The Tribes of Yahweh: A Sociology of the Religion of Liberated Israel, 1250-1050 B.C.E.*, (New York: Maryknoll, Orbis, 1979).

13 Lk 4:16-20.

14 See my 'A Liberation Image of God,' *Doctrine and Life* (February 1990) 65-68. This option, however, has to be refined substantially following the critique by feminist scholars of patriarchy, kyriarchy (Elizabeth Schussler Fiorenza) and androcentrism in Israel, and the discovery that 70 per cent of the contemporary world's economically poor are women. This contemporary phenomenon is known since 1978 as the feminisation of poverty. See my 'Women, Poverty and Christianity in Relation to Africa', *Milltown Studies* (Winter 1999) 103-129.

15 T. Dunne, Unpublished Notes.

16 The theology of liberation is a theology of this meaning and value.

17 We sometimes think that only saints have mystical experience of the Christian God, but I believe that such experience is available to anyone who is in love with this God. We can also show a lack of faith in God by not allowing for God's gift of a prophetic message and courage to people like ourselves. I use the term prophetic here in the sense of being a bearer of a transformative message from God for all the people.

18 The Jesuits subsequently sold this property.

19 A General Congregation is the highest authority in the Jesuits.

20 This way of speaking about the economically poor has become the preferred way of speaking about them in the writings of Gustavo Gutierrez. It is also a way of speaking that makes it possible to embrace others who were not to the forefront of the concern of Liberation theology at the beginning: women, indigenous peoples, etc.

Mutual Enrichment: Intercultural Spirituality in an Age of Cultural and Religious Pluralism

DR THOMAS G. GRENHAM SPS

This article explores intercultural spirituality in a context of increasing cultural and religious pluralism. From a Christian standpoint, the shape of a multifaceted intercultural spiritual vision is grounded in the historical particularity of the Christian tradition. What Christians call the gospel is shaped by a specific religious tradition, which is sensitive to enrichment among diverse cultures and religious meaning perspectives. By exploring some guiding principles and outlining a process for life-giving conversation, we can learn how diverse religious and cultural perspectives enrich the Christian spiritual worldview and vice versa. I offer two examples of intercultural spirituality from my missionary experience, which illustrate the Christian missionary task of sharing a universal spiritual vision reflected in the particularity of what Christians name as gospel. The article concludes by offering some practical suggestions for developing worldwide, life-giving, intercultural spirituality.

What is Intercultural Spirituality?

Discerning what precisely constitutes an authentic intercultural spirituality is complex. The criteria to determine a life-giving spirituality, which transcends cultural and religious boundaries, are difficult to articulate. Such an articulation is limited to historical cultural particularities and the interpretations of various religious traditions. As I understand it, an intercultural spirituality encompasses a holistic approach to understanding deep human desires across every cultural and religious boundary. The hunger for love and belonging is grounded in specific core needs, which are essential for an integral human personhood. Such needs revolve around significant friendship, meaningful activities and a sense of an ultimate reality. Consequent upon this understanding, a holistic spirituality envisions that every person is an embodied spirit with a bodiliness that is crucial for uncovering a life-giving sense of the sacred.

Every person yearns for life, meaning and a sense of dignity. People everywhere search for values like fraternity, solidarity, freedom, justice, peace, reconciliation, and healing. These shared values are understood and embodied diversely within the specificity of cultural and religious traditions. An intercultural spirituality recognises the integrity of religious and non-religious traditions to transmit meaning and life, authenticity and relevance, not only for themselves, but also across religious and cultural boundaries. Such a diverse, integral spirituality has a capacity to go beyond its historical particularities to give way to a universal or shared vision. This is an evolving process which I name *spiritual interculturation*. [1]

Figure 1

Spiritual Interculturation

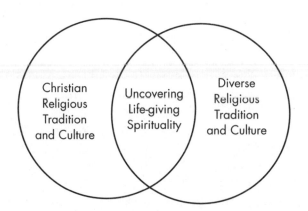

Spiritual interculturation proposes that diverse cultural worldviews and religious perspectives encounter each other to be informed and enriched. Such enrichment is observed in collaborative social, political, economic, and religious interactions. These interdependent arrangements uncover and affirm spiritual gifts for the benefit of all creation. Spiritual interculturation envisions that we view 'truth' as shared and reciprocated in the midst of religious pluralism and cultural diversity.[2] Shared 'truth' can be understood as that which is 'life-giving' within individual persons, cultures, and religions. These life-giving aspects, including principles and ideals such as goodness, love, forgiveness, generosity, justice, knowledge, peace, compassion, healing, and beauty, form the foundations for an inclusive and transformative spirituality. Such a spirituality emanating from diverse religious and cultural contexts may reflect universal cosmic influence upon the entire world. This universal cosmic penetration can be more fully imagined and appropriated through an intercultural encounter between different cultures and religious worldviews (see figure 1).

Personal Experiences of Intercultural Spirituality

I have chosen two examples that particularly highlight for me the nature of spiritual interculturation. Intentional or focused conversation emerges as the paradigm for meaningful transformation in these vignettes. The first example looks at intercultural spirituality evolving from within my own Irish context. I was born in Ireland and baptised soon afterwards a Roman Catholic Christian. Ireland was predominantly a mono-cultural and mono-religious country for most of my youth in the sixties and seventies. There was little personal critical reflection upon what I believed and why I believed in the Christian worldview. Not until I left Ireland around the mid-eighties did I become challenged and subsequently enriched through my ministry in a multi-cultural and multi-religious parish in London, England. There, in an inner-city parish, I began to explore new possibilities for my Christian faith, my cultural identity, and my sense of meaningful spirituality.

For me, the beginning of an intercultural spiritual consciousness emerged in a specific, striking pastoral encounter with a Jamaican, Caribbean Christian woman who lived in the same parish. Requested by the parish priest to visit this woman, who complained of being tormented by the spirit of an ancestor, I responded. Jacintha (not her real name) did not attend church and I secretly wondered whether she could be Christian. I duly went to minister to Jacintha, bringing some candles, holy water, and a copy of the Christian burial ritual. The parish priest suspected that her 'possession' might be something to do with a dead close relative. In an atmosphere of hospitality and conversation around a small table, I quickly ascertained from Jacintha's responses that her mother had died two years previously. There seemed to have been what I call some 'unfinished business' in the relationship. There was a framed picture of her mother hanging on the wall. I asked that this picture be placed on the table. Two candles were lit and placed beside the picture. A relaxed, conducive atmosphere was created in order to pray.

I proceeded in this candlelit atmosphere to allow Jacintha some time to talk about the life of her mother and her relationship with her. Soon it became apparent that Jacintha had a painful relationship with her mother and she regretted some things she had said and done. Jacintha seemed to find consolation in unburdening herself throughout her sharing. In the end, I suggested that we could, in our imaginations, lay her mother to final rest. So I read out loud the prayers of burial from the rite of Christian burial. I had hoped this would help, though her spiritual experience of life and death seemed different from my beliefs concerning the dead and life after death. At her request, I generously sprinkled herself and every corner of her home with holy water which visibly gave her peace of mind and considerably lowered her anxiety.

From my understanding of Jacintha's Caribbean culture, the spirits of the dead ancestors have great power over the living members of the family. If a relationship becomes strained or there is little time to repair damage in a close relationship before someone dies, the dead ancestor can become a destructive presence in the spiritual life of the living person. I learned from this experience that the task of any intercultural spirituality is to transcend particular cultural and religious boundaries. I felt in that moment I had transcended my own mono-cultural and mono-religious Irish Catholicism. From within my own Christian vision, I discovered I had a capacity to reach out to Jacintha who was grounded in her Caribbean religious worldview. Her deep religious convictions empowered me to embrace a transcendent spirituality reflected both in the Christian and Caribbean religious worldviews. I discovered that an intercultural spirituality is not about reducing diverse religious traditions to reflect my own cultural and religious sense of authentic spirituality. Rather, the ultimate aim was to offer hope and spiritual healing within the ambit of human and divine interaction reflected through the interchange between the Christian and indigenous Caribbean culture and religion.

My second occasion of intercultural spiritual enrichment took place in my later ministry among the Turkana nomads of north-west Kenya. This was an interreligious encounter between what I professed and practised as a Christian and the religiosity of the indigenous Turkana spiritual worldview. Within the crucible of a rich encounter between Christianity and the Turkana religion, I discovered a rich spirituality already present and active. For example the use of Christian oil for anointing the sick and dying was not particularly meaningful for the Turkana, rather, for them the generous application upon the body of precious white clay referred to as *emunyen* caused the release of special forces of healing. *Emunyen* had far more 'spiritual power' in the healing ceremony than the oil Christians administered. Oil is not unfamiliar to the Turkana people, but it is mostly associated with beautification and not healing.

The special white clay, which comes from a particular sacred mountain in the area, can be applied during reconciliation services. The clay is powerful especially at the beginning of Lent. In constructing an intercultural spirituality for both Christians and the Turkana in this particular Kenyan and African context, the symbolic Turkana *emunyen* and the Christian symbol of the cross interact to reflect the need to understand suffering, to heal broken relationships, to recognise human finiteness, and to seek forgiveness. Amid the interpretation hope breaks through to cast a light upon human frailty. Using specific symbolic elements within the Turkana religious cultural experience in conjunction with Christian symbols reflects a spiritual interculturation that is life-giving for all in that context. These symbols have the power to transcend human experience through a conversational dynamic conducted between the believers of two diverse religious traditions. Such an appropriation of religious meaning is not something new in the history of Christianity's encounters with new cultures and religions. The Christian biblical tradition offers many illustrations of an intercultural spirituality.

Biblical Foundation for an Intercultural Spirituality
The Syrophoenician woman's encounter with Jesus in the region of Tyre (Mk 7: 24-30; Mt. 15: 21-28) is one powerful episode of mutual intercultural spiritual enrichment. Having temporarily broken off his ministry in Galilee, Jesus crossed into the region of Tyre. He wanted no one to know where he was staying (Mk 7: 24). However, there must have been some Jewish people living around the city of Tyre for Jesus to be able to go there in the first place. A Syrophoenician woman who happened to hear that Jesus was in the vicinity shattered the secret nature of Jesus' visit. She called out to him in public to heal her sick daughter. In an instant, the woman had crossed boundaries. Interestingly, and in contrast to Jesus' encounter in Samaria (Jn 4: 1-42), it was not he who engaged publicly with an unfamiliar culture, but the

woman. The Syrophoenician took the initiative in an intercultural and interreligious process that ultimately led to the breakdown of the alleged irreconcilable differences between them.

This extraordinary intercultural encounter exemplifies the way in which Jesus became transformed through contact with a 'Gentile' or 'pagan', Syrophoenician woman. Being labelled a pagan meant she had no significant religion. Not only is Jesus' Jewish religious tradition challenged, but the patriarchal structure surrounding Jesus' own culture, reinforced by his religious tradition, is called into question. Jesus, described as 'Saviour of the world' (Jn 4: 42). will be redefined in this encounter, as will the significance of an inclusive, non-gendered God. The Syrophoenician had no direct traditional link with Judaism unlike the Samaritan woman at the well who shared a common religious heritage. This forced the issue of whether or not the spirituality that Jesus came to share could be for others, especially non-Jews.

Not only must Jesus overcome his cultural and religious bias in this context, he is also confronted with a gender boundary that challenged embedded assumptions regarding women and their faith experience.[3] The scene reflects for the world a reality that crossing cultural and religious boundaries demands an internal capacity to engage complex issues. Intercultural encounters involve a range of interpersonal circumstances which require a particular sensitivity in order to bring about mutual respect, understanding and healing.

Theologian Gundry-Volf points out that, 'there was a history of economic and political oppression of Jews by the cities of Tyre and Sidon. The Galilean back-country and rural regions around Tyre, where Jewish farmers could be found, produced most of the food for the city-dwellers.'[4] This situation was a longstanding bone of contention for the two communities. In times of shortage the city dwellers had enough wealth to buy and store food, while the peasant Galileans experienced persistent hardships. Such a provocation may explain why Jesus, a Jew, might keep his distance and desire secrecy. Jesus' hostility toward the woman only reinforces this status quo. Scripture scholar Gerd Theissen observes that,

> Jesus' rejection of the woman expresses a bitterness that had built up within the relationships between Jews and Gentiles in the border regions between Tyre and Galilee. The first tellers and hearers of this story would have been familiar with the situation in this region, so that, on the basis of that familiarity, they would

have felt Jesus' sharp rejection of the woman seeking his help to be 'true to life'.[5]

There was a constant threat of political expansion from the cities of Tyre and Sidon into areas around Galilee.[6] Such a fear would probably have been on Jesus' mind and would have reinforced his desire not to be recognised in Tyre. Though the woman must have been aware of these threats and dangers, she was courageous enough to come forward and take a considerable risk to initiate the conversation. In contrast to the Samaritan woman at Jacob's well (Jn 4:1-42), the Syrophoenician woman initiated the conversation with Jesus when she cried 'Sir, Son of David, have pity on me. My daughter is tormented by a devil' (Mt 15: 22). These were not words of threat but words of pleading for help from the Jewish stranger. Her request was for compassion upon her and her sick child rather than to intimidate Jesus. Despite the Syrophoenician woman's privileged city background, she was a humble woman who had suffered much stress because of her daughter's illness. She may have been a Hellenist Greek who spoke the Greek language. She could have belonged to the upper class in Tyre because, according to Judith Gundry-Volf, 'Hellenisation had had the greatest impact among the upper class.'[7] Even so, this did not preclude her from engaging a Jew.

In Matthew's account, when the woman begs Jesus to have pity on her he ignores her completely, not saying a word (Mt 15: 23). Jesus' disciples have to urge him to respond to the woman's plea. Jesus explains his reticence by replying with 'I was sent only to the lost sheep of the house of Israel' (Mt 15:24). Such a response indicates that Jesus had considerable difficulty moving beyond the confines of his own religious tradition. He must have thought that his ministry was primarily among his own people. Was Jesus thinking that true salvation only came from the Jews and therefore this foreign woman could not be saved?

The relational inequality of Jesus' harsh words when he said 'The children should be fed first, because it is not fair to take the children's food and throw it to the house-dogs' (Mk 7:27) leaves a lot to be desired. Dogs enjoyed little respect in the Jewish culture. Jesus had discriminated against the woman's cultural background because she was not of the same ethnic culture and religious tradition. The conversation should have ended right there with this egregious insult to her personal dignity, but it did not. Instead, the conversation continues with the woman's intuitive, and perhaps witty, response, 'but the house-dogs under the table can eat the children's scraps' (Mk 7:28). In this way the Syrophoenician makes something clear to Jesus about his own limited cultural and religious context. Through her response, she opens a window for universal spiritual transcendence.

The Syrophoenician woman's inner capacity to allow Jesus space to recover from his rash judgement and regain his equilibrium was amazing. The 'good news' already present and active in her became a lightning rod for Jesus to heal her daughter. Jesus must have grown in his own faith because of this woman's authentic spiritual perseverance. The woman had tremendous insight into herself and her religious perspective and was thus empowered to teach Jesus something about himself.[8] Jesus had become a student who had to learn about resolving his own embedded prejudice in order to reach out to heal and save beyond the specificity of his religious tradition .[9] Theissen notes:

> The Syrophoenician woman accomplishes something that for us today seems at least as marvellous as the miracle itself: she takes a cynical image and 'restructures' it in such a way that it permits a new view of the situation and breaks through walls that divide people, walls that are strengthened by prejudice.[10]

This biblical encounter between Jesus and this 'foreign' woman facilitated an intercultural engagement that served to enhance and give witness to the universality of God's gospel. A life-giving spirituality emerged that healed people despite cultural and religious divisions.[11] How is such an intercultural spirituality awakened? How do people perceive the interconnectedness of this spirituality within a contextual web of interdependent human relationships?

An Intercultural Spiritual Awakening

The answers to these questions are grounded in the work and writings of well-known Brazilian educator Paulo Freire. He posits that cultural empowerment revolves around a principle that people are conscientised, or awakened, to the reality of who and how they belong within their own unique history.[12] This wakefulness is foundational for shaping participants in specific cultures toward mutual and reciprocal spiritual interculturation.[13] Participants in cultures must be empowered to maintain and integrate the uniqueness of their historical particularities as well as learn how to go beyond them for the benefit of all creation.

Conscientizacao was the nucleus of Freire's educational worldview in reaching personal and communal freedom.[14] It became a form of learning that critically reflected upon the social, political, religious, and economic paradoxes and privileges that oppress, alienate, limit, and marginalise.[15] Anthony Gittins offers an insightful definition of conscientisation in relation to the spirituality of Christian mission. He contends that

> conscientisation, the process by which our boundaries are shaken and our sensibilities shocked, is catalytic for further change within ourselves. It is therefore a potential step to conversion. Conscientisation is the softening up of our hardened perceptions or philosophical positions; it is the breaking down of obsolete and unnecessary defences.[16]

For Christians a new cultural and religious awakening began with the reforms of Vatican II. A fresh openness to other religious worldviews and their spiritualities emerged. The document *Nostra Aetate* began a process of seeing a ray of truth in other religions.[17] The momentum initiated by the Second Vatican Council continues and much progress is being made with dialogue and conversation among the religions of the world. An effective intercultural spirituality in an age of religious and cultural pluralism demands an openness and an inner personal and communal capacity to collaborate. In light of my missionary experiences, I propose six guiding principles for Christians pursuing an intercultural spirituality.

Principles for an Intercultural Spirituality

1. It is crucial that the pastoral agent/religious educator/spiritual director maintains a conviction regarding his or her own religious tradition within every context. That is to say, understanding one's own cultural and religious history and roots is important and necessary.
2. Mutual respect and collaborative partnerships are essential ingredients for sharing spiritual values. This means agents of the Christian gospel need to recognise life-giving elements contained in any culture and religious worldview, such as the *emunyen* in the Turkana religious culture and the role of spirits in the Caribbean religious worldview. Such a life-giving and life-receiving partnership can enrich the transcendent spirituality of all.
3. Listening and providing a compassionate advocacy with those who endure great social economic and political injustices, can create a

space where the poor can feel empowered. An environment of listening created by spiritual representatives gives the disenfranchised an opportunity to find their voice and articulate their need for belonging on their cultural, political, economic, and religious terms.

4. There needs to be a kenosis on the part of any evangeliser who shares a spiritual vision: an emptying out, a letting go of preconceived ideas, biased ethnocentricities, and stereotypical opinions. This provides space for the other to participate from their vision of spiritual truth knowing that no one has a monopoly on what is true in some objective sense.[18]

5. There will be some conflicts in the process of developing an intercultural spirituality. An awareness of how to deal with personal and communal conflict is quintessential for all to grow and be transformed in a meaningful way.

6. Christian spiritual agents, as guests in diverse cultures, need to cultivate a manner which illustrates an awareness of beliefs about cultural and religious inclusivity, religious fundamentalism, world citizenship, and economic globalisation. For effective faith sharing, these agents need to embody an ability to live among and work with people from diverse cultures; walk and journey with them taking care that their own attitudes and actions are not patronising, exploiting, or dehumanising.

A life-giving spiritual interculturation requires that Christians and others holding diverse religious worldviews learn to have meaningful conversations for the well-being of the world. The principles outlined offer a broad vision for all engaged in the important task of life-giving conversation. I suggest six evolving segments that a focused conversation might take in addressing a particular need within a collaborative intercultural spirituality.

Characteristics of an Intercultural Conversation

1. The first phase of the conversation initiates and centres the process in a safe, non-threatening environment. Drawing on Paulo Freire's notion of generative themes, particular topics provide a focal point for participants within a particular culture.[19] This is the initial *centring* phase. The themes are chosen by the participants and are evoked through shared interests such as the quest for peace, the alleviation of poverty, the overcoming of political oppressions, the search for empowerment, the issue of

corruption, the yearning for religious meaning, the search for authentic spirituality, and so on.

2. The participants effectively *engage* and *name* the religious, political, economic, psychological, and social impact of a particular issue. Naming helps those reflecting to make sense of their human experience in a particular historical, cultural, and religious milieu. Participants name who they are and how they belong within their culture and religious experience.

3. For the process to evolve further, the facilitator nudges the group gently forward into the third stage by asking participants to critically reflect upon their lived experience. This reflection may be on the participants' experience of some form of spiritual oppression or aspects of an experience that brings them joy and fulfilment. Particular questions are placed before the group and an opportunity given to critique what is particularly life-giving or life-restricting about aspects of their traditions. Responses from the participants are written down.

4. The participants explore aspects of their religious traditions which inform their lived experience. For example, if the generative is the discrimination of women, for Christians aspects of Jesus' life can be discussed in which he respects the dignity of women. Other participants can access their traditions to offer helpful insights for promoting and sustaining women's dignity.

5. A time for personal and communal appropriation within the evolving conversation allows participants to integrate, on their terms, life-giving elements within their different religious traditions. For example, in relation to the two personal examples I gave earlier, how can the veneration of the spirits of ancestors be life-giving for both Christianity and the Caribbean religious worldview? In what ways does the use of *emunyen* for the Turkana offer healing and reconciliation in a process of spiritual interculturation locally and globally?

6. Finally, participants are encouraged to come to a decision for a vibrant spirituality both inside and outside their communities of faith. Making a decision for a life-giving spirituality brings people to a greater receptivity, understanding, and clarity for an intercultural and inter-religious action within the community (See figure 2).

Figure 2

The Evolution of an Intentional Conversation

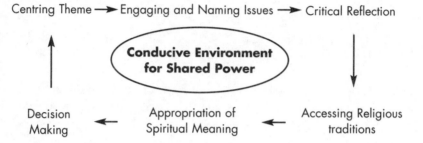

In the conversation process, people are engaged for the mutual exchange of gifts in the form of knowledge that leads to humanising transformation. Respectful conversation has the capacity to evoke life-giving spirituality and to facilitate mutual understanding. In relation to European and African Christians, theologian Paul Knitter suggests that

> More concretely, only in the actual, on-site conversation can European and African Christians determine whether the condemnation of polygamy is a demand of the gospel or a reflection of Western family structures. Such a protracted, open-ended process can make Christians who have never known any other Christianity than the present one very uncomfortable and fearful.[20]

The Challenge for Christian Intercultural Spirituality

Having outlined briefly how a focused conversation might evolve, I do not wish to be naïve and think that such interfaith and intercultural conversations would proceed without challenge. In relation to Christian spirituality generally and theological reflection particularly, one of the greatest challenges is to find an appropriate starting point or a frame of reference in which to begin a process of discerning God's activity in people's lives. For Christians in an age of pluralism, this discernment transpires within the social, religious, and physical environment of lived human experience. Within a specific historical, religious, and cultural context, the process of making accessible the traditions of the community for guiding the process of personal and collective transformation toward God is essential.[21]

A life-giving intercultural spirituality is challenged to offer meaningful ways in which diverse religious perspectives and their spiritual traditions are accessed for mutual enlightenment and enrichment. For Christians, the Christian tradition is appealed to for the complete disclosure of the gospel embodied in the person of Jesus Christ.[22] The challenge for the Christian worldview is to discover the vision of the gospel already present and active in every person, culture and religious experience. In a new era of economic globalisation, various religious evangelisers are challenged to attend to the reality of the spiritual dimensions of diverse cultural and religious traditions. Consequent upon this attentiveness, a special relationship emerges between the evangelisers in which the problems of the world are tackled and resolved.

Opportunities for Christian Intercultural Spirituality

An intercultural spirituality offers opportunities for Christians and adherents of other religions to collaborate for peace, justice, and reconciliation in the world. Whether one is a Christian or non-Christian, conversation can be a paradigm to mutually discover life-giving truths about what it means to be human. Such conversations offer the possibility for a spirituality of shared empathy in responding to the suffering in the world. This empathy is fostered as a result of personal and communal formation in a shared diverse world.

Both religious and secular education play important roles in forming the minds, hearts and actions of participants motivated to foster a life-giving spirituality. An intercultural education provides further opportunities to ensure that Christian intercultural spirituality is vibrant and relevant. Though every religion and culture promotes particular absolute and exclusive claims of truth, an intercultural spirituality provides opportunities to shape new religious structures and institutions that tackle social, political, economic, and religious problems locally and globally. Thus, the exclusiveness of religious and spiritual particularities is superseded.

Conclusion

This chapter has explored the prospect for an effective intercultural spirituality for the well-being of all. The practical implications of this spiritual vision for the world rely on (1) the pledge by diverse cultures and religions to mutually discover a life-giving spirituality, (2) the shaping of inclusive structures for meaningful conversation to share faith, (3) the construction of contextual theologies within a safe environment of religious arrangements, and (4) the collaboration of religious traditions.[23] Such suggestions, if implemented, can create a new dawn for Christian spirituality.

Notes

1   For more details regarding the concept of interculturation, see T. G. Grenham, 'Interculturation: Exploring Changing Religious, Cultural, and Faith Identities in an African Context' *Pacifica: Australasian Theological Studies*, 14/2(2001), 191-206.

2   Ibid., 193.

3   See D. Hampson, *Theology and Feminism* (Cambridge, Massachusetts: Basil Blackwell, Inc., 1990) 148-175. Hampson discusses her views on the particular way the image of God has been conceived and shaped in the Christian tradition. She examines the 'the projection of a masculinist construal of reality' which has excluded feminine qualities from the shape of God.

4   J. Gundry-Volf, 'Spirit, Mercy, and the Other', *Theology Today*, 51 4(1995), 516.

5   See G. Theissen, *The Gospels in Context: Social and Political History in the Synoptic Tradition*, Trans. Linda M. Mahoney (Minneapolis, MN, USA: Fortress Press, 1991) 65.

6   Gundry-Volf, 'Spirit, Mercy, and the Other', 517.

7   Ibid., 516.

8   S. Van Den Eynde, 'When a Teacher Becomes a Student: The Challenge of the Syrophoenician Woman (Mark 7. 24-31)' *Theology* 103/814 (2000), 274-279 at 278.

9   Ibid.

10   Theissen, *The Gospels in Context*, 79-80.

11   Theissen, *The Gospels in Context*, 80

12   P. Freire, *Pedagogy of the Oppressed*, revised 20th-anniversary edition, (New York: Continuum: 1995) 17-18. Freire, refuting allegations that conscientisation leads people to 'destructive fanaticism,' suggests that the process makes '... it possible for people to enter the historical process as responsible Subjects, conscientizacao enrols them in the search for self-affirmation and thus avoids fanaticism.'

13   M.J. Collier 'Reconstructing Cultural Diversity in Global Relationships: Negotiating the Borderland' in *Communication and Global Society*, eds. G-M Chen and W.J. Starosta, (New York: Peter Lang Publishing, 2000), 215-233. From a sociological viewpoint, Collier's objective is to 'uncover ways in which we make sense of our diverse cultural identities and bring to light through discursive consciousness a clearer understanding of how we construct relationships across and within borders.' She proposes dialogue as having the ability to 'contribute to decolonialisation by providing concrete examples to open up spaces for understanding and emancipation,' 232.

14   P. Freire, *The Politics of Education: Culture, Power, and Liberation* (Massachusetts: Bergin & Garvey, 1985) 160. Freire describes the conscientisation process as 'cultural action for freedom.'

15   P. Freire, *Education For Critical Consciousness* (New York: Seabury Press, 1973) 19.

16   A.J. Gittins, *Bread For the Journey: The Mission of Transformation and the Transformation of Mission* (Maryknoll, NY: Orbis Books, 1993), 61.

17   *Nostra aetate*, No. 2.

18   P.J. Palmer, *The Courage to Teach: Exploring the Inner Landscape of A Teacher's Life* (San Francisco: Jossey-Bass, 1998) 104. Palmer suggests that '...the only "objective" knowledge we possess is the knowledge that comes from a community of people looking at a subject and debating their observations within a consensual framework of procedural rules.'

19   Freire, *Pedagogy of the Oppressed*, 84-90. In relation to the role of a focusing activity in his methodology of shared praxis, see also T.H. Groome, *Sharing Faith: A Comprehensive Approach to Religious Education & Pastoral Ministry* (San Francisco: Harper, 1991), 155-174.

20   See P.F. Knitter, *Jesus and the Other Names*, 153.

21   M. Boys, *Educating in Faith: Maps & Visions*, (Kansas City, Missouri: Sheed & Ward, 1989), 193.

22   L. Swidler and P.Mojzes (eds.), *The Uniqueness of Jesus: A Dialogue with Paul F. Knitter* (Maryknoll, NY: Orbis Books, 1997) 164. He asserts that most 'religions that have survived the centuries have traditions within them that call their followers to respond to the terrestrial needs of others.' This means they are concerned with the well-being of those who suffer and who are oppressed.

23   T.G. Grenham, 'Reconstructing Christian Culture toward the Globalization of Gospel Vision: Identity, Empowerment, and Transformation in an African Context' in *Missiology: An International Review*, at 31/2 (2003), 236.

Trailing the Spirit: An Approach to Applied Spirituality Research

Dr Bernadette Flanagan PBVM

One important aspect of the current debate around the nature of the discipline of spirituality concerns the specific methodologies that are appropriate to its tasks. No broad consensus has yet emerged around this issue, but it may be that this diversity enriches the quest for methods adequate to tracking the uniquely diverse ways in which the Spirit inspires, motivates and sustains the desire to live in God. In this essay I will outline a three-phased approach that I have found useful to investigate the sense of God amongst an inner city community in Dublin. First I will outline the method in an abstract form. Towards the end I will illustrate the use of the method with a small sample of data.

The Stages of Trailing

It has already been noted that many aspects of the contemporary experience of spirituality are not documented. In order therefore to create an initial description of the lived experience of spirituality amongst people today it seems necessary to begin by listening to personal accounts of that experience. Since the focus of the type of studies in spirituality that are envisaged by this author are centred on personal spiritual experience, qualitative rather than quantitative data seems central to the research project. Secondly, because the data reflects the intensely personal character of each individual's appropriation of spirituality, a heuristic approach to analysing the data seems best suited to attending to the unique emphases of respondents. Thirdly, while respecting the individual character that each person's account of spiritual experience assumes, the aim of such studies in spirituality would ultimately be to tentatively identify some common strands in these experiences so as to develop the first draft of an ethnographic profile of religious sensibility amongst a particular population of people. The aim of the next three sections is to outline the presuppositions and nature of qualitative research, heuristic description and ethnographic profiling.

Mapping the Footprints: Qualitative Research

The phrase 'qualitative methodology' refers in the broadest sense to research that produces descriptive data, and so findings are primarily communicated in words rather than numbers. Recording descriptive observations, conversations and other qualitative methods are not contemporary inventions. It was not, however, until the early twentieth century that what came to be termed as 'qualitative methods' were commonly employed in research[1]

The distinctiveness of qualitative methodology is perhaps most evident when it is contrasted with the quantitative approach. The latter has been more commonly employed to investigate the religious dimension of Irish spirituality up to this time, as is evident in studies such as those of Micheal MacGréil, SJ.[2] In examining the place of religion in the life of Irish people information was collected on how often the subjects prayed, their attitudes towards Christian unity, their disposition towards priesthood and religious life and how they perceived the importance of religion to 'getting on' in life. Interviews did not vary from a set of prescribed questions, nor were there follow-on questions used to probe the actual issues and life-circumstances lying behind individual answers. While the information generated by the questions asked did illuminate certain narrowly-defined patterns of religious practice and attitude across a large population, it did not offer depth of insight into the way religion structures, forms, influences and gives meaning to particular persons' lives. Neither did it probe the extent to which persons actually lived in ways consistent (or not) with the answers they gave

A qualitative approach, on the other hand, offers the opportunity to explore in some depth and detail the sensibilities, hopes, values, beliefs or lived practice of a smaller number of people. Since spirituality today is a rich, diverse, multi-faceted phenomenon the openness of qualitative research is well suited to respecting its complexity.

While quantitative research methods are 'etic', assuming an outsider's point of view; the 'emic', or insider's perspective, is central to qualitative inquiry.[3] This terminology was developed in 1954 by the American anthropologist Kenneth Pike. He suggested that a researcher, instead of forcing pre-designed categories on data (etic), ought to search instead for categories used by the interviewees. The contrasting epistemologies operative in these approaches also shape the purpose of each method. Quantitative researchers seek a sufficiently large sample to create generalisations that will predict responses amongst other persons and groups. In contrast qualitative researchers regard it as their role to depict accurately and interpret how a group of people understand particular aspects of the world around them.

These assumptions and purposes shape in turn the approach any inquiry in spirituality today might assume. Qualitative researchers will seek to construct simple problem statements (such as 'What music or life experiences have spiritual significance for you?') and a small number of initial questions (such as 'Has music, a film, a friendship, a tragedy ever changed your sense of God?'). They will then proceed to explore these questions through individual or group interviews. Conversation is an ancient form of obtaining knowledge as is evident in Socrates' use of dialogue for philosophical enquiry. The constitution of knowledge through conversation has been a subject of interest to the contemporary philosopher Richard Rorty. He contends that '(k)nowledge (is) a matter of conversation and social practice rather than an attempt to mirror nature'[4] The emphasis on conversation as a mode of knowing may be particularly strong in postmodern philosophy because of the loss of faith in an objective reality that could be mapped in scientific models and from renewed interest in the place of discourse and negotiation in the construction of the meaning of lived experience.

A qualitative research interview will seek to cover both a factual and meaning level. It will aim to hear what is explicitly said and what lies 'between the lines' by describing what has been picked up and checking it out with the interviewee for confirmation or disconfirmation. This focus on precision in description and stringency in meaning corresponds in qualitative interviews to exactness in quantitative measurements.[5] When an interviewee's response is ambiguous, what matters is to describe precisely the ambiguity, having clarified it as far as possible, since the aim is not to gather unequivocal and quantifiable meanings of the theme being explored, but to adequately reflect the world of spiritual meaning within which the people interviewed live.

The contrast hinted at above between quantitative and qualitative methodologies highlights how different assumptions, purposes, approaches, roles of researchers and investigative procedures underpin each of these two modes of inquiry. While the former method is supported by a positivist paradigm the latter is more interpretative, perceiving the world as socially constructed, complex and ever-changing.[6] These characteristics arise from the influence of symbolic interactionism on the development of qualitative methods.[7] Symbolic interactionists emphasise that the same symbols and texts can be experienced differently by people because of life experience, age or the social situation in which they find themselves. They emphasise that it is often the interpretation of experiences and situations that shapes the living practice of spirituality then rather than norms, values and goals.[8] The conversation, reported at the end of this article, about the Gospel story of the widow's mite eloquently illustrates this truth.

In reporting the findings a limited use of matrices, charts and other displays may be undertaken by qualitative researchers in order to allow the reader see more clearly connections in the data gathered in the interviews. However the rich descriptions of interviewees have a quality of undeniability that make their un-edited reporting the most central feature of this type of research. 'To know a rose by its Latin name and yet to miss its fragrance', stated Eisner, 'is to miss much of the rose's meaning.'[9] To attend to the forms of meaning constructed in the stories of others requires of qualitative researchers a capacity for empathic understanding.[10] They may not assume the detached and impartial stance of quantitative investigators.

In general then I want to suggest that a qualitative methodology may be especially fruitful for studies of contemporary spirituality which, (1) seek to offer an initial, focused examination of the spiritual experience of living persons, (2) draw their primary data from a relatively small number of individuals, and (3) intend to understand the actual, rather than the ideal, influence and function of a spirituality in peoples' lives.[11]

Lying in Wait: Heuristic Inquiry

The second step in this approach to spirituality research will be to attend more deeply to the gathered data. Heuristic inquiry is distinctive in that it seeks to pay particular attention to the personal character of the data. Heuristic analysis also consciously includes the researcher's own experience within the framework of the study. In this way it may be considered as an extension of spiritual accompaniment into the public forum.

Central to heuristic methodologies are certain presuppositions regarding of the nature of cognition. Philosophers such as Bernard Lonergan[12] and Michael Polanyi[13] establish the foundations for employing the post-Kantian, post-positivist understanding of the cognitional process that is advocated in this approach to research in spirituality. Their insights regarding cognition begin from an appreciation of the nature and structure of knowing itself, rather than the nature and structure of reality (phenomenology) or that of language (hermeneutics). Though little has been done by way of comparative analysis between Lonergan and Polanyi their strong epistemological compatibility has been noted.[14]

Lonergan's interest in cognitional theory between 1940 and 1953 found expression in *Insight*. One of the fundamental characteristics of knowledge for Lonergan is that it is heuristic.[15] One seeks to arrive at the unknown by anticipating acts of insight and by conceptually expressing those insights. The lines of inquiry continually shift as the anticipated solution is continually refined. Thus the heuristic notion becomes more precise. Cognition then is not a single act or even a system of static steps. Rather it is a process that is 'self-assembling and self-constituting'.[16] In this way, Lonergan views knowing as inherently personal. That such a view also informs the cognitional theory of Michael Polanyi is evident in the title of his work *Personal Knowledge*. The key to Polanyi's theory of knowledge is the premise that he wrestles from common experience, that we know more than we can tell. On this basis he distinguishes 'tacit' and 'explicit' dimensions of knowing and insists on the logical dependence of explicit knowledge on the tacit.[17] Dynamic tacit knowing yields personal knowledge. It has three closely related and interwoven aspects. It begins in an understanding that is constituted by hunches and surmises which cross a logical gap. It then progresses to 'participating feelingly in that which we understand'.[18] Polanyi insists that any attempt to depersonalise knowing will inevitably produce an alienation of the known from the knower.[19] The journey finally leads to 'appreciation'.[20] When a solution is claimed to be found, the intellectual excitement, which is what he calls appreciation, carries the knower on with a craving to verify the claims made. Heuristically, the questor is impelled by intellectual passion to new frameworks of interpretation in pursuit of discovery:

> Intellectual passions do not merely affirm the existence of harmonies which foreshadow an indeterminate range of future

discoveries, but can also evoke intimations of specific discoveries and sustain their persistent pursuit through years of labour. The appreciation of scientific value merges here into the capacity for discovering it; even as the artist's sensibility merges into his creative powers. Such is the heuristic function of scientific passion.[21]

It is evident then from Lonergan and Polanyi's use of the term 'heuristic' that it is a mode of cognition that emphasises the subjective process of reflecting, exploring, sifting and elucidating the matter under investigation. Also, whereas phenomenology and hermeneutics might lose the persons interviewed in the process of descriptive analysis, in heuristics the research participants will remain visible in the examination of the data and will continue to be portrayed in their own right,[22] rather than as instances of a phenomenon.

In turning to the Greek origin of the word heuristic, from which the popular term 'eureka' is derived, two forms of the root are particularly significant. *Heurisko* describes the activity of discovering, while *heurikon* refers to a principle of discovery.[23] These two forms are the basis for Lonergan's distinction between 'heuristic notion'[24] and 'heuristic structure'.[25] The heuristic notion is the enveloping drive that carries sense and imagination to understanding, judgement and knowledge, through the dynamic process described by Lonergan and Polanyi above. A heuristic structure on the other hand is a procedure which guides the arrival at knowledge of the unknown.

The idea of heuristic structures (that is, heuristics) has appeared sporadically in the literature of philosophy and logic to describe the methods of inductive reasoning.[26] As well as being guided by Lonergan and Polanyi's heuristic notion of the cognitional process, studies in spirituality may also employ a heuristic structure. I have found that one, developed by Clark Moustakas in the field of humanistic studies of experiences such as anger, loneliness, despair and hope, may be particularly helpful for processing qualitative data gathered in contemporary studies of spirituality.

In his comprehensive account this heuristic structure Clark Moustakas has identified seven of its characteristic features and six phases in its execution. The central feature of heuristic analysis, according to Moustakas, and the concept which underlies its operation is 'tacit knowing'.[27] It calls the researcher to be open to being guided into unrecognised directions and sources of meaning. This will occur due to a movement from an *initial engagement* with a topic through processes of *immersion* and *incubation*. In the case of a research project in spirituality the initial engagement will occur through taking time in the environment of the people being studied and observing and listening for their implicit religious awareness. Immersion then occurs in the process of interviewing while the incubation will extend over subsequent months when there will be an effort to let go of the details of the interviews in order to get an interior sense of the broad picture of the interviews as a whole. The period of incubation 'allow(s) the inner workings of the tacit dimension and intuition to continue to clarify and extend understanding on levels outside immediate awareness'.[28] Heuristic inquiry will involve disciplined commitment to follow the subjective past ordinary levels of awareness, living the questions internally, recording hunches and ideas as they emerge, and consulting with others regarding these incipient insights.

The turning point in a heuristic inquiry is what Moustakas has termed *'illumination'*.[29] This moment is well illustrated in a story by Bernard Lonergan in his already mentioned major work *Insight*,[30] where he recalls Archimedes

> ... rising naked from the baths of Syracuse with the cryptic cry 'Eureka'. King Hiero, it seems, had had a votive crown fashioned by a smith of rare skill and doubtful honesty. He wished to know whether or not baser metals had been added to the gold. Archimedes was set the problem and in the bath had hit on the solution. Weigh the crown in water! Implicit in this directive were the principles of displacement and specific gravity.

This story illustrates how while Archimedes' illumination or insight built upon his understanding of scientific principles, he also had to be open and relaxed to see the essence of truth. This suggests that the awakening is most likely to occur when the researcher is able to be open to a degree of creative spontaneity, without intense concentration. Thus any attempt to rigidly superimpose prior categories on the data has to be resisted. Rather the aim will be *'explication'* and *'creative synthesis'*.[31] This will involve articulating and clarifying the significant findings of the interviews (explication) and formulating these findings into an ultimate representation of the phenomenon which is been investigated (creative synthesis).

In conclusion it is appropriate to note the suitability of heuristic inquiry for exploring issues in contemporary spirituality. The unexplored nature of many phenomena in contemporary spirituality, which are currently being researched, mandates a discovery, investigative approach. This immediately suggests the necessity for a heuristic notion to underpin the inquiry and a heuristic structure to guide it, since these studies will be concerned with what is new, rather than what is familiar. A methodology for attentive listening, like that developed by Moustakas, is also essential to employ since much research in spirituality today will be initial studies of previously un-researched populations or phenomena. The fact that the subject of many of the studies will be an experiential reality, suggests the appropriateness of an instrument of inquiry drawn from the human sciences.

Taking the Picture: Critical Ethnography

While qualitative methodology focuses on the question of *what* data will be gathered and heuristics determine *how* this data will be processed, we must now turn to the question of *why* these steps might be taken. In many studies the aim will be to investigate the spiritual experience of a particular group of people who represent a distinct strand of contemporary spirituality, such as persons living with a life-threatening illness, members of the travelling community or composer/performers of spiritual music. Ethnography is the terminological description of this aim.[32] Ethnography originated at the beginning of the last century from the work of Franz Boas in America and Bronislaw Malinowski in England.[33] It was developed within anthropology to help researchers describe aspects of the way of life of a particular group of people. Ethnography had its origins in an intellectual response to the neglected underclass of Chicago's socially disadvantaged urban ghettos. It sought to move away from a value-laden view of cultural diversity, which defined that which differed from the mainstream as pathological, to a position which allowed marginal groups in society speak for themselves.[34]

A key defining feature of ethnography is that it is concerned with the ordinary and everyday rather than the extraordinary. The ethnographic researcher seeks however to notice what is exceptional and unique in the quotidian life of a distinct population. So while traditionally anthropologists had been concerned with making the exotic 'familiar' the ethnographer tried to make the familiar 'strange'.[35] The success or failure of ethnography depends on the degree to which it rings true to those whom it seeks to represent. While it is possible that those represented may disagree with the researcher's interpretations and conclusions, it is important that they should recognise the details of the descriptions as accurate.

While some ethnographic accounts conclude by describing what is, others go further and investigate why this is so. Thus the distinction arises between 'conventional' and 'critical' ethnography respectively.[36] Critical ethnography attempts to situate the interpretations and understandings in the group investigated within a broader setting. It sees meaning as cultural or structural. It believes that group phenomena, including manifestations of spirituality, do not operate in an isolated fashion, but are affected by all sorts of trends in society. Cultural realities are a central synthetic concept governing studies in critical ethnography.

Walking the Trail

One final question will probably be 'does this schema work?' I would like to respond by taking an illustration from my own research experience. It will follow the stages described above in reverse vis-à-vis a key insight arrived at in my efforts to understand the central dynamics of the sense of God amongst the residents of Dublin's inner city, the Liberties.

After four years of living with the research data I came to realise that a central ethnographic characteristic had the power to unify much of what had been gathered. This insight consisted in realising that in the community of inner-city Dublin *God has been revealed in suffering*. Just as Israel's understanding of God was born out of the Exodus, so the pervasive experience of suffering shaped the distinctive way God was approached in the Liberties. Suffering assumed the great multiplicity of forms in this community that is characteristic of the modern inner-city. Yet God was not presumed to have forsaken the people of the Liberties. Rather, God was sensed in those who lived with the losses, the pain and the desperation – the homelessness, drug addiction, violence and imprisonment that was so prevalent.

Following one story from the interview data through Moustakas' stages of heuristic enquiry led to an insight regarding the central place of suffering poverty in understanding the religious experience of people in the Liberties. A woman who had been interviewed told an event from her childhood: 'It was the time for the Easter dues. A priest from the parish called to enquire why no dues had been paid for some time. On the day in question my mother's resources came to just one small coin, which she had left out on the mantelpiece to pay for a loaf of bread. My mother protested her poverty asking what she'd give her children to eat if she had no money to buy bread. But the curate didn't listen and he left, taking the coin with him for the dues. When he went out the door my mother just sat down and cried because that's all the money she had.'

Echoes of the biblical story of the widow's mite (Mk 12:41-44) resounded for me in the conclusion of the story. This story of the widow's mite had occurred in an earlier interview and so I went back to look at the raw material (qualitative data) of the interview again. It was again a woman interviewee and she had put the question: 'what's the real meaning of the widow's mite story (Mk 12:41- 13:2) if you take it for starters that God doesn't want people to be hungry? If it means that you have to give your last penny in a collection then that's only for people with plenty of money. They can go to the "hole in the wall" and get more. I think Jesus is giving out about the widow being so stupid with her money.'

Following a decision to be rigorous in using the data, I approached a colleague in the Scripture Department with the puzzle that had been put to me. He pointed out that while the vast majority of interpretive work done on this story has, in the past, as the interviewee suggested, focused on the widow's exemplary financial generosity, he said Addison Wright's interpretation was a helpful exception. According to Wright, the Temple context is essential to the proper understanding of the story. He suggests that just as Jesus points out that the Temple is soon to be overturned (v. 2) so it will be recognised that the widow's contribution was made to an institution in decline and so not to be imitated. [37]

Thus, in my own account of the living spirituality of native residents of Dublin's inner city I found that the research framework based on ethnographic profiling, heuristic attentiveness and qualitative data took me into uncharted waters and yielded results that time and the pastoral responses of others have served to confirm.[38] I can only conclude by recommending, 'take and try'.

Notes

1   Qualitative methods first became popular in the period 1910 to 1940 when researchers in social studies associated with the University of Chicago produced detailed participant observation studies of urban life. Ibid., 3-5.

2   M MacGréil, *Prejudice in Ireland Revisited* (Maynooth: Department of Social Studies, 1996) deals with religious practice in general. Part three of section three of Chapter Six specifically looks at the Irish experience of 'closeness to God'.

3   R. Sands, M. McClelland, 'Emic and Etic Perspectives in Ethnographic Research on the Interdisciplinary Team', in E. Sherman, W. Reid, eds, *Qualitative Research in Social Work* (New York: Columbia University Press, 1994) 32-41.

4   R. Rorty, *Philosophy and the Mirror of Nature* (Oxford: Blackwell, 1980) 171.

5   S. Kvale, *InterViews: An Introduction to Qualitative Research* (London: Sage, 1996) 32.

6   R. Rist, 'On the Relation Among Educational Research Paradigms: From Disdain to Detente', *Anthropology and Education Quarterly* 8(1977) 42-49.

7   P. Maykut, R. Morehouse, *Beginning Qualitative Research: A Philosophic and Practical Guide.* 'The Falmer Press Teacher Library, 6' (London: Falmer Press, 1994) 3.

8   The development of symbolic interactionism by Charles Horton Cooley, John Dewey, George Herbert Mead and others is traced in M. Kuhn, 'Major Trends in Symbolic Interaction in the Past Twenty-Five Years', *Sociological Quarterly* 5(1964) 61-84.

9   E. Eisner, 'On the Difference Between Scientific and Artistic Approaches to Qualitative Research', *Educational Researcher* 10/4(1981) 5-9 at 9.

10   S. Kvale, op. cit., 35.

11   C. Glesne, A. Peshkin, *Becoming Qualitative Researchers: An Introduction* (London: Longman, 1992).

12   B. Lonergan, *Insight: A Study of Human Understanding* (London: Longmans, Green and Co., 1957).

13   M. Polanyi, *Personal Knowledge: Towards a Post-Critical Philosophy.* 'The Gifford Lectures, 1951-1952'. Revised. (New York: Harper & Row, 1958).

14   J. Kroger, 'Theology and Notions of Reason and Science: A Note on a Point of Comparison in Lonergan and Polanyi', *Journal of Religion* 56(April 1976) 157-161; Idem, 'Polanyi and Lonergan on Scientific Method', *Philosophy Today* 21(Spring 1977) 2-20 and E.T. Kumfer, *Lonergan and Polanyi on Cognitive Meaning.* 'Unpublished Doctoral Thesis' (Carbondale: Southern Illinois University, 1982).

15   B. Lonergan, *Insight*, 114.

16   B. Lonergan, 'Cognitional Structures', *Continuum* 2(1964) 530-542 at 531-532.

17   M. Polanyi, 'Science and Religion: Separate Dimensions or Common Ground?', *Philosophy Today* 7(1963) 4-14 at 5.

18   M. Grene, ed., *Knowing and Being: Essays by Michael Polanyi* (Chicago: University of Chicago Press, 1969) 148-149.

19   M. Polanyi, *Personal Knowledge*, 253.

20   Ibid., 143.

21   Ibid.

22   This emphasis on singularity is inspired by the work of the French philosopher Julia Kristeva. Since 1980 the tenor of Kristeva's work has changed. She has left behind elaborate attempts to develop a general theory of the subject and language and

turned instead to the analysis of specific personal and artistic experiences, experiences which might at the same time offer a deeper understanding of social and cultural life. Her studies have explored the experience of love – *Tales of Love*. Trans. L.S. Roudiez (New York: Columbia University Press, 1987); the experience of depression – *Black Sun*. Trans. L.S. Roudiez (New York Columbia University Press, 1989); and the experience of being a foreigner – *Strangers to Ourselves*. Trans. L.S. Roudiez (New York: Columbia University Press, 1991).

23   B. Lonergan, in E. Morelli, *Understanding and Being*, 74.

24   B. Lonergan, *Insight*, 380

25   Ibid., 68.

26   R. Nickerson, et al., *The Teaching of Thinking* (London: Lawrence Erlbaum Associates, 1985) 74.

27   C. Moustakas, *Heuristic Research*, 22.

28   C. Moustakas, *Heuristic Research*, 29.

29   Ibid.

30   B. Lonergan, *Insight*, 3.

31   C. Moustakas, *Heuristic Research,* 30-32.

32   The developing use of ethnography in spirituality research is evident in T. St James O'Connor, et al., 'Making the Most and Making Sense: Ethnographic Research on Spirituality in Palliative Care', *The Journal of Pastoral Care* 51/1(1997) 25-36.

33   M.D. LeCompte, J. Preissle, *Ethnography and Qualitative Design in Educational Research* (New York: Harcourt Brace Jovanovich, 1993) 4.

34   J. Thomas, *Doing Critical Ethnography*. 'Qualitative Research Methods, 26' (London: Sage, 1993) 11.

35   M.D. Lecompte, J. Preissle, op. cit., 3.

36   J. Thomas, Ibid., 4.

37   A. Wright, 'The Widow's Mites: Praise or Lament? – A Matter of Context', *Catholic Biblical Quarterly* 44(1982) 56-265.

38   B. Flanagan, *The Spirit of the City: Voices from Dublin's Liberties* (Dublin: Veritas, 1999)

PART TWO

Case Studies

Visited by God: Spirituality and the Irish Immigrant Community

PAULINE CAMPBELL RSC

On return from a sabbatical in the United States in 2001, I found myself in a discerning process for a changing ministry. During these months, I came in contact with refugees and asylum seekers through a voluntary organisation called Spiritan Asylum Services Initiative (SPIRASI)[1]. It was an experience that left an indelible mark on my life, it was a journey into a 'new territory' for me, and perhaps for others. My background was in nursing, a structured ministry, so the challenge of change met me at every angle.

I came from a background of a hospital where patients had all the comforts of everyday living. One of my first assignments was to assess the bathroom facilities of a survivor of torture living in a ground-floor flat; he had many physical disabilities from his past experience. I was shocked by what I experienced. A pipe had burst in the upstairs flat just over his bed; all he had to collect the dripping water was a plastic bag, his bedclothes were drenched and there was no heat to dry them. It took many phone calls to the landlord to sort out the problem. This landlord was receiving a generous rent from the Department of Social Welfare. On another occasion when I visited an asylum seeker/survivor of torture in a hostel, I discovered I could not see her in her one room as she had two small children. The only place I could speak to her was in the hall, which was fitted with microphones and a camera. There was no way that this woman could speak freely to me about her past or present needs.

As I walked with these strangers I discovered so many things both in myself and in their relationship with me; I felt I would like to understand their lives more deeply.

I made a list of questions that everyone working with recent immigrants should ask themselves:

- How important is confidentiality in their lives, especially for survivors of torture?
- Trust is a major issue. They know nothing about me; how can I gain their trust?
- What really sustains them from day to day? How is their dignity as human persons affected by the decisions of our government not to allow the breadwinner of the family to work?
- Some people must wait for years to hear about their future, though their children are happily settling into the Irish education system. How do they keep their religion, spirituality and culture alive in their children who are attending Catholic schools?
- How do the Church and the Irish people receive people of other faiths? How do we practise hospitality to the stranger? Are we able to see and accept the talents and gifts of those who have been involved at a ministry level in the Church of their native country and who are longing to be part of the Church here but feel outside it?
- Is there a neighbourly relationship and a welcome in the rural communitites and the housing estates for the refugees who are not accustomed to the Irish culture and ways of living?

Refugees and Society

It could be argued that these strangers have provided the first real litmus test to our cosy self-image as a warm, friendly and welcoming people, an image of the Ireland of the thousand welcomes, the *céad míle fáilte* that has been carefully cultivated and exported.

I found in my own personal life that the refugee could teach me to become detached from material possessions and from being self-centred. Their insecurity and uncertainty about their future challenged me not to rely merely on myself or on human planning. Many of their cultural values and simple dignity as human beings reminded me that a persons' worth is determined by what he or she is rather than what one has. Society today often fails to honour all its members, because it does not value and cherish people for what they are – images of God – but rather values them for the wealth they possess, the power they can exercise. Consequently, those who are refugees, who may have neither riches nor honour are devalued, considered worthless and unless they have great inner strength, can come to experience themselves as worthless. When we consider Christ's relationship to God, which he expressed in his human relationships through a life of sharing, a life for others, we are challenged to this same life choice in our relationship to other human beings. One of the many challenges we have to face is that the riches of this world are for the benefit of all human beings irrespective of race, religion or culture. Where have the Irish people buried that beautiful gift of compassion for others and neighbourliness that has been so much part of our heritage, I wondered?

As I walked with the immigrant community in their journey of homelessness, their openness and generosity so often challenged me to share with them all that I have and am. A Muslim survivor of torture who was a stranger to me recently residency received status. I, a stranger, was invited into his family to celebrate with much generosity, openness, warmth and trust. This change in circumstance perfectly illustrates that, as Balasuriya says, 'humanity must find peaceful and just means of adapting a new paradigm in which human beings are more important than the national frontiers ... We are called to transcend our narrow particularities in order to arrive at a higher, wider and a deeper level of sharing among all human beings.'[2] If we are to take these attitudes to heart, we need leadership both from our Church and our government leaders to accept the stranger into our culture and to be able to give witness to the world of living out true Christian values.

The Global Situation

The description of refugees by the United Nation High Commission for Refugees (UNCHR) states: 'Owing to a well founded fear of being persecuted for reason of race, religion, nationality, membership of a particular group or political opinion, is outside the country of his nationality and is unable, or owing to such fear, is unwilling to avail himself of the protection of that country.'[3] The UNHCR is mandated by the United Nations to lead and co-ordinate international action for the worldwide protection of refugees and the resolution of refugee problems. It strives to ensure that everyone can exercise the right to seek asylum and find refuge in another state and to return home voluntarily.

In order to try to understand the refugee situation I was meeting around family meals I had to look at the globalisation of the world economy and communication systems. This is being accompanied by growing polarisation between the richest and the poorest people leading to increased – often forced – global migration. It could appear that

'Fortress Europe' is being reinforced to stem a 'foreign invasion'. Yet as European citizens we have contributed to the forced migration. The refugee phenomenon is a consequence of international trading patterns and cannot be addressed in isolation from this.

The challenges set for Europe and Ireland by modern migrations into Europe are new. We frequently tell ourselves that Irish emigrants were an asset to the countries they entered. Can we admit, as Irish Europeans, that today's strangers have a similar contribution to make to the quality of Irish and European life?

The Irish Churches

One of the first groups of modern refugees admitted to this country came from Hungary in 1956. It turned out to be a disaster with the main issue being the right to work. Today, we still have the denial of the right to work while the application for asylum is being processed. This leads to exclusion from mainstream society. Once again, I ask whether we are failing as Christians to take the challenge of the Gospel to heart? Would Gospel principles urge us to further the recruitment of ethnic minorities within public agencies? Would the Churches be able to give leadership in actions to change our society from a mono-cultural to multi-cultural focus including integration of refugees into our parishes and communities? We are being challenged to build a future that is not based on polarisation, but in which differences are reconciled and integrated. The former director of the Irish School of Ecumenics, Geraldine Smith has said that, 'rather than intensifying the burden of pressure and guilt, Churches need to be more modest and self-limiting in their expectations'.[4] The Churches must exercise leadership in offering understanding and guidance. There are many gems within statements from the Irish Catholic Bishops on asylum-seekers and refugees but they need to be fleshed out and applied at parish level. They urge society not to view new arrivals as a threat to cultural identity and well-being but to view this time as an opportunity to walk together with people rich in unique gifts. Unless these words are enacted at parish level in, for example, liturgical worship and committees, it could be like the seed that falls on waste ground.

The traditional shape of Irish spirituality is undergoing a profound change. With the arrival of people from other cultures and diverse Christian traditions, the Christian Churches in Ireland are challenged with new opportunities and new responsibilities. If culture is viewed as an expression of the richness of human nature, it allows us to look beyond the differences to realise that all people share the same common humanity, the same basic needs and desires. Each of us is born into a culture and our way of life is culturally shaped from the moment of birth. In clinging on to their own cultural identity, refugees' way of expressing their humanity may be strange to Irish practices and values. All need to find the deeper common humanity in order to forward integration.

There are many questions and challenges being presented at parish level. Are we asking the stranger: What do you want? What do you need? What is your story? The Church is a place where nurturing an awareness and exchange of cultures can take place. We ask what we have that we really want to share? Roddy speaks about these people: 'They bring the richness of an expression of faith, worship and social concern which reflect the culture and history of their fatherland. The Church communities here have to be open to receive; the Christian Churches are challenged by the Word of God to "widen the space of your tent", (Isa 54:2).'[5]

Co-operation among the communities of faith will lead to new advances in the search for and creation of a deeper unity of the Christian family. Church action can in turn be a leaven for a dialogue of action directed towards the wider human family. To move out of the spiritual comfort zone, to be willing to live with ambiguity is to leave space for something new to emerge. The Christian community be a healing, reconciling and moderating agent in a new way in society?

In 2002 the Irish Council of Churches undertook a research project conducted by David Stevens into the religious life of the refugee within Protestant, Orthodox and new Churches. It did not include the Catholic Church.[6] It looked at the basic facts regarding the fast rate of development of new Churches and the issues related to these developments. These include the religious life of these Churches, their pastoral and practical needs, their relationship with 'mainstream' Irish Churches, the possibilities of linking these Churches to ecumenical structures. In his study Stevens found that mainstream Churches have only developed to a limited extent from the influx of Christian immigrants to Ireland during the 1990s. While some ministers have been enthusiastic about welcoming these strangers and sympathetic towards their integration into the faith community, others have been resistant. Many immigrants who have joined black majority Churches in Ireland initially worshipped in a mainstream church, but felt they were not welcomed or accepted.

Femi Olayisade, is a researcher who is supported financially by Christian Aid to carry out the work on Nigerian Churches. He is a member of Elim Pentecostal Church. He found that black majority churches, many of them established by people of Nigerian origin, are now a substantial presence in many towns all over Ireland, partly because of the government's asylum seekers dispersal policy.

He found seventy-two different African Churches – mostly Pentecostal – established in Ireland. Why the proliferation of Pentecostal churches? One of the pastors Lawrence Oyetunji from Nigeria, said: 'I believe the Lord is planning a change in Ireland, that's why there are a lot of Pentecostal churches. I believe God wants to use us. In the past Irish people went to Africa and sowed a seed. Now the seed they sowed is the fruit that is manifesting here. It's a part of what they brought. We have come with the gospel of our Lord Jesus Christ and with the Holy Ghost and Fire.' He went on to say how saddened his heart is when he sees the old and retired people in mainstream Church, but not the youth.

Welcoming the Stranger in Gospel Challenge

In order to discern God's work in this new social development of welcoming immigrants it is fruitful to turn to Biblical texts to recover an ancient inspiration. There we search for the challenge to live up not only to our humanitarian ideals, but also our Christian ideals. The theme of care of the stranger is woven into the whole tapestry of God's relationship with humanity in the Judeo-Christian revelation.

In the New Testament, hospitality emerges in meetings and transactions with strangers. The command to 'love ones neighbour' expresses the essence of the Christian message. In his ministry and teaching Christ makes welcoming the stranger a criterion for salvation. The Kingdom of God reigns in partnership, in co-operation in companionship, in building God's house together. The love of Christ challenges all to break through boundaries established by religion or nationality. 'Our hearts must be broken open, until our hospitality and compassion match those of God'.

Hospitality: The Irish Welcome

Home is central to the human experience, not simply as a place but as a state of being. 'Home is where the heart is' and it is a symbol of identity, belonging and origin. If leaving home is a forced process, the loss takes on a profound character: loss of roots, of a sense of history, of sense of place. Homelessness is spiritually traumatic. John O'

Donohue answers the question why we need to belong: 'It is the desire so deeply rooted in every heart. It is the nature of the soul to belong; it can never be separate. It is the vital principle of one's individual life. It weaves into a tapestry of spirit that connects everything everywhere.' As humans we are linked to one another like mountain climbers on a steep ascent – irrespective of beliefs or spirituality – in the common struggle to grow and be wise, to learn and to love, to build a home.

As I travelled with the stranger, I heard these words frequently: 'We often feel isolated, marginalised. The Churches do not know our language, culture or history, but we do want to be welcomed, respected and valued.' There is a great need for us to be aware of people's cultural homelessness and for having this acknowledged and engaged. Can we open our doors and spaces to the human cry of the refugee? New life will be brought to the Churches in Ireland if they can open themselves to this moment of challenge and opportunity.

The Dignity of Work

The most soul-destroying aspect of life for an asylum-seeker (on direct provision in hostel-type accommodation) is the boredom, frustration, waiting for a decision on their application for refugee status. These people's attempts to adjust to a life of relative idleness result in a great deal of dissatisfaction, listlessness, psychosomatic disorders, depression, short tempers and negative functioning in the life of the whole family. While the role of the father changes when pregnancy occurs within the family, so that he has to take the children to school, do the shopping and cooking, this is totally against the culture for the male to be involved in domestic work.

Work is a vital expression of creativity and the human spirit though it is not everything in life. Edward Sellner outlined the value regarding work that emerges in the creation story: 'initially the work of God is the work of creation; secondly, humanity is the culmination of that creation, everyone made in God's image shares the same power to create; thirdly, the myth of the creative process of God was not completed or brought fully to fruition until the rest on the seventh day.' This pattern of interconnectedness of work and leisure also reveals a rhythm of work and rest that is good for humans.

More recently John Paul II's *Laborem exercens* affirmed the Christian understanding of work as being a good thing for humanity as it transforms nature, but it also achieves fulfilment for the human being.

Community, Worship and Celebration

The preaching of Jesus contained a double challenge. It insisted that those who work for the coming of God's Kingdom would live by patterns of equality in social, economic and political relationships. His message also challenges those promoting justice and right relationships to look at the stranger with new eyes, to see the inherent and inalienable dignity and worth of each person: 'I tell you solemnly, in so far as you did this to one of the least brothers of mine, you did it to me'(Mt 25: 40).

John Paul II in his message for World Migration Day (1996) said: 'the responsibility to offer hospitality, solidarity and assistance lies first of all with the local Church. She is called on to incarnate the demands of the Gospel, reaching out without distinction towards these people in their moment of need and solitude.' The presence of a stranger in the midst of the community can undermine the comfort of the familiar and force the worshipper to confront the unknown. As a community gathered in worship, we need to examine our sense of community and inclusiveness.

T.R. Whelan in his article 'Racism and Worship in Ireland', says 'that we need to "hear the story" of the stranger this being part of the "God-story"'.[7] What a challenge it would be to hear the refugee tell their story in our Churches, how they feel they are being accepted or rejected. The call to communion at the level of our common humanity challenges all members of the Church. Simple grace-filled outreach to newcomers on the part of all the members of the Church community is a first step that needs to be accompanied by a constant and patient effort at intercultural communication.

A statement of the US Catholic Bishops, 'Welcoming the Stranger Among us, Unity in Diversity' says, 'The Church of the twenty-first century requires a profound conversion in spirit and in its institutions to reflect its own cultural pluralism. It will be a Church of many cultures, languages and traditions, yet simultaneously one as God is one Father, Son, and Holy Spirit ... unity in diversity.'[8] Are we able as Irish followers of Christ to take on this challenge, as it is here to stay?

Sharing Spirituality: Personal Testimony

I have been privileged in the last two years to walk with three immigrant survivors of torture.

Asabe was reared and educated as a Muslim. After becoming a Catholic in her late teens, she lost her right arm through torture. After the torture, the New Testament came alive for her and she felt drawn to serving God while attending a Missionary secondary school. She married a Catholic and left her country. Since coming to Ireland she has found the Catholic Church unwelcoming. Her heart is better able to express its gratitude for being accepted as a refugee in a safe country in an Episcopalian Church. Her husband, **Ifrani**, also a Catholic, is struggling and in a dark place. 'I feel I am an outsider in the Catholic Church. I find it unwelcoming, only a few are involved in the liturgy. Quite often the handshake at the Kiss of Peace has not been offered to me. I feel that the people control the timing of worship; the Mass is so rushed. What I miss most of all is participation in the Church in professing my faith and support in passing it on to my three children. In my home country I was totally immersed and involved in the Catholic Church. Sunday worship was always the pinnacle of my life with my family.'

Joy, a mother of five children lost a leg from torture. Presently she is struggling to live with a sixth pregnancy and an abusive husband. She was a member of the Pentecostal Church in her home country: 'Religion meant nothing to me until the experience of torture. I had a religious experience when left to die on the roadside by my perpetrators; I felt I was deeply loved by God. With the multiple difficulties in my life I feel that God has sustained me to survive to look after my children, He is a loving God. There are times when I have nobody to trust or to talk to but Him. I pray in my home with the children.'

From these stories we see that the refugee's choice to practise religion has to be made and remade in their new situation with its tensions, uprootedness and resettlements. Accompanying these challenges are loneliness and the inability to express oneself in a newly-learnt language. The parish community is a place where the stranger and locals can get to know each other and be transformed into a community by being part of a shared worship. In sharing faith with others, each is challenged in spite of cultural differences, to consider the stranger as brothers and sisters, sons and daughters of the one God. The Irish Catholic Bishops' Committee on Asylum Seekers calls out: 'if we allow ourselves to be enriched by those who are cultural, ethnic and whose religious background is different from ours; in confronting this choice our Christian faith is clear. It calls us unequivocally to create a more welcoming, more inclusive society, a society prepared to share its increasing wealth, resources and opportunities with others.'[9] Let us encourage each other to cross the barriers of racism, to celebrate the dignity and worth of the human person irrespective of race, culture or religion and to be a witness to the coming of the reign of God in a new way at this time.

Notes

1. SPIRASI is a service providing medical and psychosocial services for survivors of torture, multi-level English language training geared towards integration, multi-level computer training to bridge the digital divide, facilitation for immigrant artists and exhibitions of intercultural art, partnership projects at local, national and international levels, research and publication on refugees issues and outreach support services.

2. See J. Roddy, 'Refugees and Asylum Seekers in Ireland' in *Studies* 91/364 (Winter 2002) 328-337 at 328.

3. The Office of the United Nations High Commissioner for Refugees was established on December 14, 1950. To date the agency has helped an estimated 50 million people restart their lives. See www.unhcr.ch.

4. G. Smith, 'Is Modern Ireland Losing its Soul?' in *Doctrine and Life*, 53/4 (2003) 205-214 at 209.

5. J. Roddy, 'Refugees...' *Studies*, (Winter) 2002, 328-337 at 334.

6. D. Stevens, 'Research into Aspects of the Religious Life of Refugees, Asylum Seekers and Immigrants in the Republic of Ireland' (11 September 2002) published by the Irish Council of Churches.

7. T.R. Whelan, ed., *The Stranger in our Midst, Refugees in Ireland: Causes, Experiences, Responses* (Dublin: Kimmage Mission Institute, 2001).

8. National Council of Catholic Bishops, USA, *Welcoming the Stranger Among Us* (2000)

9. *Refugees and Asylum Seekers – A Challenge to Solidarity*. An updated Joint Policy Document of The Irish Commission for Justice and Peace and Trócaire together with Statements on Asylum and Refugee Issues by the Irish Bishops' Committee on Asylum Seekers and Refugees (1999-2001).

The Spirituality of L'Arche and Faith & Light Communities

BRÍD FITZGERALD

For the past eighteen years I have been involved in a community called Faith and Light. This is an international movement for people with intellectual disabilities, and their families and friends, who meet on a regular basis to spend time together in activities and in prayer. By sharing our stories and lives together, we build relationships and as a community we welcome the opportunity to celebrate and go on pilgrimages and outings with other communities.

Faith and Light is a sister movement of the residential L'Arche communities, and shares the same spirituality and ethos, which is rooted in gospel values. Thus there are strong links between the movements, both founded over thirty years ago. They have grown worldwide and welcome people from all races and creeds and spirituality remains an essential and grounding part of the movements. The very fact that these communities have continued to grow and flourish is evidence that they are meeting and fulfilling needs that exists for those who come to spend time and to share their lives and stories together.

L'Arche

In 1964, Jean Vanier, inspired and encouraged by his friend and spiritual director Père Thomas Philippe, OP, began to share his life with two men with intellectual disabilities: Raphael and Philippe. He bought a small house in the village of Trosly-Breuil, near the forest of Compiègne, France. He called the house 'L'Arche', ('The Ark' –the logo of L'Arche is a boat with three people in it.) There they shared their lives together as a family and became the first L'Arche community. Friends came to help in the community and more men with disabilities were welcomed. Despite the growing-pains of the early days, working through them in a spirit of prayer and deeper understanding of the ministry of Jesus in the gospels, the little boat moved on and grew in a spirit of humility, simplicity and joy in each other. Vanier often speaks of those early days together: 'They led me into a world of friendship and communion which was healing me and bringing me new life... They needed me to be with them, to love them and to establish relationship with them.'[1]

L'Arche welcomes people with learning disabilities into a home to live with people who come to share their lives with them and to build community together. Some assistants come for periods from three months to two years. Some stay longer and others choose it for life. Vanier explains: 'a community is not simply a group of people who live together and love each other. It is a current of life, a heart, a soul, a spirit. It is people ... who are all reaching towards the same hope.'[2]

He tells us that 'a community isn't just a place where people live under the same roof: that is a lodging house or hotel. Nor is a community a work team. Even less is it a brood of vipers! It is a place where everyone ... is emerging from the shadows of egocentricity to the light of love.'[3] This journey from egoism to love takes time, for a heart to move from the attitude of the 'community for myself' to that of 'myself for the community and the community for God and those in need'. It is a path of sacrifice, of shedding our own defences, of truly encountering and overcoming our own pain and weakness, our helplessness in the face of another's pain.

Faith and Light Community
Faith and Light was founded by Jean Vanier and Marie-Hélène Mathieu in Lourdes in 1971, following a pilgrimage with 1,300 people with learning disabilities and their families and friends. For approximately eighteen months the pilgrims had been meeting regularly to prepare for the trip by building community together in a spirit of prayer and friendship. This pilgrimage was inspired by the story of the pain suffered by Camille and Gerard, parents of two boys with severe disabilities who had experienced rejection.

Faith and Light is a community movement. At the heart of these communities are people with a more or less serious intellectual disability: children, adolescents and adults. They are surrounded by their family and friends, especially young people. These communities are usually made up of about thirty people. A Faith and Light community meets regularly (usually once a month) in a spirit of sharing, celebration and prayer.

Faith and Light gives to the persons with intellectual disability the possibility of recognising and using their gifts and discovering the joy of friendship. To parents and family members it gives support and helps them to better appreciate the inner beauty of their children. It calls siblings to appreciate that a person with a disability can be a source of life and unity. 'If this person disrupts their life, he/she can also transform and transfigure it.'⁴ The people who come as friends discover that there is another world besides that of competition and materialism; they are invited by those who are weak and deprived into a world that listens, a world of tenderness, loyalty and faith. We sometimes speak of all being in the same boat and the Faith and light logo is a boat containing a large number of people under a cloudy sky, which has the sun bursting through. It was designed by a person with intellectual disability and inspired by the story of Jesus asleep in the boat. (Lk 8: 22-25).

The Spiritual Vision of Jean Vanier
Jean Vanier speaks of L'Arche as a family created and sustained by God and this implies a sharing of one spirit, one vision and one spirituality. He defines spirituality as 'a way of life that implies choices and a particular ordering of priorities'. While the gospel is the source of Christian spirituality there are many ways to live out its message. Just as the gospels tell us the stories of the life and message of Jesus, so too, in L'Arche and Faith and Light, we are encouraged to share our personal stories, and to be attentive to them. When we hear stories of special moments or key experiences we celebrate them and they help us to deepen our spirituality and commitment and keep the vision of the movements alive. Stories help us to grow in wisdom and can transform and heal us.

Vanier says that 'the spirituality of a disciple of Jesus is a spirituality of incarnation, the word made flesh' it cannot to be seen as a flight from the body. He sees Christian spirituality as 'a concrete reality. It is a power or a spirit that will help us make certain transitions, transforming us in the love of Jesus, making us other Christs, bringing us closer to the Father and to others.'⁵ In this way we are invited to grow from a world of selfishness and negativity to truth, reality and wisdom, to openness, vulnerability, to caring, and to heartily welcoming people who are different, people who are in pain and poverty. He adds: 'spirituality is always for love; it is growth in love. And this growth ... comes through the bonding with the poor person who in a particular way is chosen and loved by God'.

Worldwide there are many inter-faith communities of L'Arche and Faith and Light where Hindus, Muslims and Christians are welcomed, and each person is rooted in his or her own religious tradition. Vanier reminds us of Gandhi's spirituality; God is to be found in the poor, rejected and marginalised people and by entering into a covenant of love with them we become closer to God.

This spirituality could be called a 'spirituality of littleness' since through the reality of being with the 'little ones' we are learning from them and discovering our own littleness. In the words of Teresa of Avila: 'fix your eyes on the Crucified and everything will become small for you' (*Interior Castle*, VII, 4.8).

The L'Arche/Faith and Light Model of Spirituality

The Charter of the Communities of L'Arche states that 'L'Arche communities are places of hope. Each person, according to his or her own vocation, is encouraged to grow in love, self-giving and wholeness, as well as in independence, competence and the ability to make choices.' Among the fundamental principles outlined in this Charter is the acknowledgement of the common humanity of all people, whatever their gifts or limitations. 'Everyone is of unique and sacred value, and everyone has the same dignity and the same rights, which include 'the right to friendship, to communion and to a spiritual life.' The Charter clearly states that, 'If human beings are to develop their abilities and talents to the full, realising all their potential as individuals, they need an environment that fosters personal growth.' This means living in an environment where they are valued, accepted and supported in an atmosphere of trust, security and mutual affection. 'If it is to be a healthy place where all members can grow, a great deal of living and loving, hurting and healing has to happen.'

Similarly the foundational belief of Faith and Light, as stated in the Charter and Constitution, is 'that each person with an intellectual disability is fully a person with all the rights of a human being: above all the right to be loved, recognised and respected for himself or herself and in the choices he/she makes.' Furthermore, Faith and Light believes that every Christian member is called to deepen his or her life in Jesus, to receive all the spiritual richness from their Church, sacraments and liturgical tradition. However we must be practical and realistic. Vanier says that 'in community life, it is obviously necessary to have people who are in charge, people with a vision who keep the community unified.'[6] It is vital to have competent leaders, that they be elected through discernment and prayer, in the light of the Holy Spirit. Through dialogue and discernment everyone is given a voice, 'From the standpoint of efficiency ... this could seem a complete waste of time. But we discovered that it was important. It allowed all of us to clarify our choice ... it created an inner cohesion in the group.'[7] Human wisdom and competence as well as good doctors and psychologists are necessary, 'to enable us to better respond to the cry of the poor, to allow ourselves to be disturbed by them, and to announce again and again the good news of Jesus.'[8]

According to the Charter of Faith and Light, the person with disability is called to be a 'source of grace and peace' for the whole community, the Churches and for all humanity. In an ecumenical context the person who is weak and disabled can become a source of unity between Churches.

Therefore, in order to help people with intellectual disabilities to grow and to flourish, it is necessary to understand their suffering and their human needs and to be able to respond in an experienced, competent, caring way, by being fully present and 'with' them in their humanity. We must also be prepared to see them in the light of the gospel message.

The spirit of the gospel message is lived out in the mutual ministry of L'Arche and Faith and Light. This ministry is to respond to the call to littleness, to make a covenant with the poor. Those who come to 'be with' people with intellectual disabilities must come in Vanier's words 'to discover a secret, like a treasure hidden in a field, the pearl of great price ... hidden in the hearts of the poor and the lonely, the sick and the blind, in all those who are vulnerable ... they must come, as a child in wonder.'[9]

'When you are with people who suffer from mental handicaps, you cannot be in a hurry. It takes time to listen to them and understand them. Efficiency is not their strong point! They find their happiness in presence and relationship; their rhythm is the rhythm of the heart. They oblige us to slow down and enter into relationship.'[10] To reach out to others in this way is not easy, it is radical, but we must find deep within ourselves the grace to enable us. That is the gift of the Holy Spirit. The rewards are manifold. We discover that wounded people have an enormous capacity for love. They have the capacity to reveal in all of us what is most fundamental: that we too are wounded and imperfect, but, that even in our fragility we are all made in the image and likeness of God and that we are loved by God as we are.

There is the great secret and joy to be discovered by friends and assistants who come to these communities; while they often come to be active, to 'do things for' they soon discover that the person with disability simply wants real companionship and this means allowing the spirit of the scriptures to guide them.

Themes from Scripture
While the spirituality of L'Arche and Faith and Light is deeply rooted in gospel values, there are certain themes from the New Testament, which are more to the fore. Three main themes weave through the spirituality and practical lived out experience of life in these communities. Each one can be aligned to the reality of community life:

- Let the children come   *The call to littleness*
- Host and Guest   *Mutual Ministry*
- Table Fellowship   *Eucharistic Ministry*

Let the Children Come – The Call to Littleness
'God has chosen the foolish to confound the wise; the weak to confound the strong' (1 Cor 1:27).

In the synoptic gospels there are several passages where Jesus welcomes the children, the little ones, 'Let the children come' (Mt 19:13, Lk 18:15, Mk 10:13). He announces that the kingdom of God is precisely for these, for unless we become like children we cannot enter the kingdom. On the night of the Last Supper in John's gospel, Jesus addresses the disciples as 'little children' and says 'I give you a new commandment, that you love one another. Just as I have loved you, you also should love one another. By this everyone will know that you are my disciples, if you have love for one another' (Jn 13:33-35).

Jean Vanier often speaks of his own poverty and ignorance at the beginning of L'Arche and says that this very poverty helped him to be more attentive to God, to trust and to welcome God's plan. 'I am more and more convinced that God has supported and guided L'Arche over the years to reveal to society and the church the place and value of people with mental handicaps – particularly at this point in history where their lives are threatened because people are asking whether they should be alive at all.'[11]

Therefore it is important to remain open to God's plan, to avoid letting a community become too self sufficient and too secure. He often speaks of the story of the people of Israel, beginning with Abraham's faith and trust in God, setting out into the unknown to establish a new life. The people gradually grew and became strong, they moved from Abraham's insecurity and dependence on God to a security and power that could defend itself from and compete with other peoples. For L'Arche this movement from insecurity to security can be avoided if a community remains alert by remaining faithful to the little ones who cry and disturb, by being attentive to community life and by trusting in Providence. This implies wisdom and competence, reflection and prayer.

When Jesus announces his mission in Luke's gospel (Lk 4) and quotes from the prophet Isaiah, he is clearly stating his option for the poor and the marginalised. Jesus chooses not just to serve the poor, but also to become one of them. The Word has become flesh; God the Son has become a helpless child, needy and fragile.

'Whoever welcomes one of these little ones in my name, welcomes me. And whoever welcomes me, welcomes the one who sent me' (Lk 9:48) 'Jesus did not come to judge or condemn, but to gather into one all the scattered children of God (Jn 11:52). He came to break down the walls that separate the rich from the poor, the healthy from the sick, so that they might be reconciled to one another and discover that they are all part of one body.'[12] Thus we find in the gospels Jesus attracts the powerless ones, the little ones, the outcasts and the marginalised of the society and reveals God's mercy and love to them, by becoming one of, and one with them. St Paul encourages this example of Christ, the downward path of humility, and self-emptying: (Phil 2:6-8).

We live in a world that is full of superficiality and competitiveness, we are taught to be the best, success and wealth are the prime values, we learn to build up barriers to defend ourselves, to appear strong. 'To remain faithful to small things without first having made one's fortune seems regressive.'[13] Movements such as L'Arche and Faith and Light can therefore be seen as counter-cultural.

Host and Guest – Mutual Ministry

'Do not neglect to show hospitality to the strangers. For by doing that some have entertained angels without knowing it' (Heb 13:1-2).

This quotation from Hebrews reminds us to be aware in our encounters with others to look beyond the façade to the person. Too often it is in retrospect we realise the significance of a chance meeting, and we are reminded of the gospel words 'as you did it to these my brethren, you did it to me' (Mt 25:40). We are blocked by our own very human inhibitions, our busy lives and our priorities. We sometimes fail to see the value of 'wasting time' with another person and how it can be an enrichment for our own lives too. Hospitality, like other virtues, needs to be put into practice, so instead of fleeing from our own loneliness or pain, we must strive to be open to discovering the presence of God therein.

Sheila Cassidy writing in *Good Friday People,* reflects on the Fourth Song of the Servant (Isa 53:1-5) and says: 'There are people who make us want to screen our faces, to turn away, and yet it is through them that the grace of God flows to water our arid souls. These people are the hallowed bamboo through which the life-giving water flows, the reed pipes on which the musician plays his song.'[14]

Throughout the Scriptures we are reminded time and time again to be attentive: 'Let your ears receive the word' (Jer 9:20); 'I thank you, Father, Lord of heaven and earth, because you have hidden these things from the wise and the intelligent and have revealed them to infants' (Mt 11:25); 'Let anyone who has ears listen' (Mt 11:15,43; 13:9); 'Let anyone with ears to hear listen!'(Lk 14:35); 'Do you have eyes and fail to see? Do you have ears and fail to hear? (Mk 8:18). When Elijah encounters the Lord on the mountain, it is not in the magnificence of nature, not in the wind, earthquake or fire, but in the sound of sheer silence, the sound of the gentle breeze (I Kgs 19:11-13).

Hospitality is a way of being, an activity; it is an act of faith and of love, it is communication and communion. It means taking a risk, the risk of being challenged, of feeling vulnerable and the risk of rejection. Hospitality, therefore, involves being both guest and host; it is about receiving and giving.

In the gospels, Jesus is seen as both guest and host. In the familiar stories such as Luke 19:5, Jesus invites himself to dine with Zacchaeus, who receives him joyfully and is transformed through the encounter. In John 4, Jesus the guest, meeting the Samaritan woman, says, 'Give me a drink' and as host he offers her 'living water'.

Likewise, in Mark's gospel (Mk 7:26-30), Jesus may be seen as host. A Gentile woman, a Syro-Phoenician who begs him to drive a demon out of her daughter, approaches him. His first reaction is to refuse because he sees his mission as to the people of Israel and not to the Gentiles. This woman is not prepared to accept his response and while she acknowledges that the gentiles are seen as 'dogs' by the Jews, she nevertheless argues that even the dogs eat the crumbs from the children's bread. Jesus, we are told is moved by her faith, and heals her daughter. 'In recognising Jesus as the giver of bread (v. 28) she already acknowledges him as the 'one loaf' (8:14) for Gentile and Jew. Jesus bows to the woman's faith (Lk 7:9).'[15] This passage corresponds with the discovery of many who come to spend time with people with intellectual disabilities, they find their value systems turned upside down, they come to serve, to give of their gifts and talents to discover that they are the recipients of even greater gifts. They 'bow' to their teachers, the little ones and are transformed and opened up to a new reality, to a new way of being.

Table Fellowship – Eucharistic Ministry
'When you give a banquet, invite the poor, the crippled, the lame, and the blind. And you will be blessed, because they cannot repay you' (Luke 14:13-14).

In the gospels we see Jesus born in humility and living a life of beatitude, gentle, meek, weeping, persecuted, in pain and then broken and dying on the cross. We see a life lived in the loving acceptance of those who were rejected, outcast, marginalised, weak and vulnerable. In that acceptance we see the love and healing that Jesus gave, not just to the lepers, but also to the lepers of society. He chose to become one of them, to welcome, to share, to break bread, to celebrate, to help, to forgive, to wash their feet and to have his own feet washed. 'As we share the same table and become friends with people suffering from mental handicaps ... we achieve unity, reconciliation and peace. We grow in divine tenderness. We discover the forgiveness of Jesus and become a symbol of the wedding feast of heaven.'[16]

We note that in the gospel of John, the first place Jesus takes his disciples is to a wedding, a celebration of love, a banquet (Jn 2). Here, we see the first sign of Jesus, in which for the early Church 'the wine of the Eucharist would come to mind, especially since John tells us that that the changing of water to wine took place before Passover (v. 13).'[17]

The high points for the disciples during their years with Jesus were their community meals. The Charter of Faith and Light has as its first heading: 'A community which meets', simply that, not meeting to 'do', but meeting to 'be with' others. Meeting to spend time together, to talk and listen, to form personal relationships where gifts and pain are shared, meeting to support each other in friendship and fidelity, and discovering the joy and celebration that follows. Meeting to share a simple meal, breaking bread with others, the true symbol of friendship and companionship and not expecting to be repaid, that is real communion. It is too easy to be present with people we like and who like us, the challenge is to be present with those who have nothing apparent to give and the blessing comes with the discovery of the gift of recognising the face of Jesus revealed in their presence – meeting Jesus.

People with intellectual disabilities love to celebrate in an atmosphere of inclusion and joy. 'This atmosphere of joy comes from the fact that everyone feels free to be themselves in the deepest sense. They have no need to play a role, to pretend to be better than the others, to demonstrate prowess in order to be loved. They discover that they are loved for themselves.'[18]

Love is never static, ' a human heart is either progressing or regressing ... When we welcome people, we open the door of our heart to them and give them space within ... welcoming people means bringing them right into the community.'[19] While a community, family or household needs time to be enclosed and intimate it also needs times of openness and welcome. 'Life brings new life'[20] but when we welcome the stranger we take a risk and become vulnerable. 'Those who are generous are blessed, for they share their bread with the poor' (Prov 22:9).

The story of the road to Emmaus (Lk 24:1-12, Mk 16:1-8) 'is a sophisticated eucharistic catechesis: a "Liturgy of the word" followed by a "liturgy of the eucharist".'[21] The two disciples recognised the person of Jesus in the breaking of the bread and remembered the journey and how their hearts burned when he 'broke the word' with them.

The early Christian community continued the common meals when they gathered together in communion with one another bringing Jesus into their presence again. Breaking bread together became a time of thanksgiving, of Eucharist. In the Last Supper in John's gospel, before the feast of the Passover (Jn 13:1), we know that Judas is about to betray Jesus, yet Jesus does not exclude him from the table or the foot-washing. Jesus rises from the table, and begins to wash the feet of the disciples. This is a menial task, that of a servant. Jesus gives the disciples a model of mutual service and a lesson in humility and he recommends that they too must do this in memory of him. 'The washing of the feet is not first and foremost an act we all have to imitate. It reveals how Jesus is calling all his disciples to an inner attitude of service and love in all things ... in L'Arche we have discovered how important it is also actually to wash each other's feet.'[22]

As a paraliturgy, the washing of the feet has become an important aspect of the spirituality of both movements, particularly during retreats. It is a very powerful gesture, which signifies communion, love and service. In an ecumenical or inter-faith context where the celebration of the Eucharist can be a source of pain for those who are excluded, the inclusion of the washing of the feet can serve as a source of unity, enabling all to participate.

All three themes can be linked together by one word: love. Love is more than a feeling; it is a call to action. The spirituality of Jean Vanier and the movements he has founded is one grounded in the gospels, and follows the life and ministry of Jesus. He says: 'Out of love we have been created to love: to use all our energies and gifts to create a more just and loving society, where each person has a place ... to witness to the church and to the world that God knows all persons in their deepest being and loves them in their brokenness.'[23]

To love is not easy. When we embark on a relationship, we call forth a part of ourselves, that we might prefer to hide: our vulnerability. Love and friendship means trusting another by sharing what is deep within us, exposing ourselves to another, revealing that vulnerability and littleness that leaves us open – open to ridicule, rejection or exploitation, but also open to love and commitment. That littleness, that child within us in awe and wonder is crying out for relationship and at the same time afraid of it and where it might lead us. 'Love ... breaks down the barriers and protective armour we have built around ourselves. Love means letting others reach us and becoming sensitive enough to reach them.'[24] The daily routine of community life, doing the little everyday chores, which may seem valueless and insignificant 'can become gestures of love that help create a warm atmosphere in which the communion of hearts can grow. In this way, community life becomes a school of love,'[25] and those who commit to community life discover a spirituality of love through the small things.

Learning from the Lived-Out Experience

The spiritual life in communities of L'Arche and Faith and Light takes the form of a 'spirituality of littleness', rooted in the gospels, it is a spirituality of 'Beatitude' deeply incarnational and Christian.

For those of us who have embraced this spirituality, there is a discovery and a surprise that it shapes us and teaches us more about our own littleness, brokenness and vulnerability and therefore how enriching it is for our lives. We find that we receive much more than we can give or have given by being part of these movements. With this in mind, I wanted to explore this spirituality and how it impacts on the lives of others who are involved in both L'Arche and Faith and Light.

In these two movements we are encouraged to tell and re-tell the founding stories. Vanier stresses the importance of telling our own stories and of sharing them with others in order to keep the spirit and the vision of the movement to the fore.

Last year I spoke with twelve people representing both movements. These included three parents, three friends, three members of L'Arche and a chaplain. I also carried out a group conversation with five people in L'Arche in order to include two men with intellectual disabilities who are core members of a L'Arche community. The other seven participants were interviewed individually.

Having looked at L'Arche and Faith and Light from the spiritual and scriptural aspects, these conversations gave an insight into the lived out experience of those who have embraced that life and ethos. Their comments and stories told with openness and a sense of gratitude, serve to illustrate how their lives have been transformed and enriched; how people with intellectual disabilities teach us to look again at our value systems and challenge us to re-focus our priorities, to confront our own anguish and discomfort and become attentive to what this spirituality is calling us to. Clearly from the insights shared, there is a depth to this spirituality, which has brought about much reflection and has been a source of personal growth and human flourishing through love – the mutual ministry of guest and host.

I would like to highlight some points made by the interviewees to illustrate some key convictions that have become central to their lives and are integral to the interrelationship of spirituality and intellectual disability in Faith and Light and L'Arche:

• People with learning disabilities are able to get into the heart of things; they connect on the level of the heart.

- Being with people with intellectual disabilities teaches you the importance of relationship.
- It has made me more aware of who I am myself.
- My life has been put into perspective... there is no place for masks.
- Discovering that people with handicaps are just as wounded in their affectivity, they reveal your own woundedness.
- The life in L'Arche can't be an unreflected life.
- We are not just providing a service; we are building community together with people who are, in the eyes of the world, fairly powerless and helpless.
- We would have a very different world if it were based on companionship and not on competition.
- It has revealed to me the value of human life.
- These are the people who have revealed to me who I am, who God is, what the world is about.
- God's love is present in the most awful situations as well; my belief is that God is present in sadness and despair.
- The image of God as powerless is the heart of where God is at for me. A compassionate God, a God of humanity and also a God of weakness.
- When I discover the richness and the extraordinary humanity of these people and their capacity to bring out the incredible faith hope and love that is in them, I become even more and more in awe of the Creator.

Notes

1   J. Vanier, *A Door of Hope* (London: Hodder and Stoughton, 1996) 10.
2   J. Vanier, *Community and Growth* (London: Darton, Longman and Todd, 1979) 19.
3   Ibid., 10.
4   Faith and Light, *Charter and Constitution*, 4.
5   J. Vanier, *Deepening our Spirituality in Faith and Light* (Paris: 3 Rue du Laos, Faith and Light booklets, 1991) 4-5.
6   J. Vanier, *The Heart of L'Arche*, 62-63.
7   J. Vanier, *Community and Growth*, 217.
8   J. Vanier, *The Heart of L'Arche*, 8.
9   J Vanier, *The Broken Body* (London: Darton, Longman and Todd, 1988) 78.
10   J. Vanier, *The Heart of L'Arche*, 35.
11   Ibid., 74.
12   Ibid., 18.
13   Ibid., 61.
14   S. Cassidy, *Good Friday People* (London: Darton, Longman and Todd, 1991) 5.
15   W. Harrington, *Mark New Testament Message Vol. 4* (Dublin: Veritas, 1979) 105.
16   J. Vanier, *The Heart of L'Arche*, 58.
17   R. E. Browne, *The Gospel and Epistles of John, A Concise Commentary* (Collegeville: The Liturgical Press, 1988) 29.
18   J. Vanier, *Community and Growth*, 74.
19   Ibid., 195.
20   Ibid.
21   W. J. Harrington, *Luke: Gracious Theologian, the Jesus of Luke* (Dublin: The Columba Press, 1997) 106.
22   J. Vanier, *The Scandal of Service, Jesus Washes Our Feet* (London: Darton, Longman and Todd, 1997) 8.
23   J. Vanier, *The Heart of L'Arche*, 8-9.
24   J. Vanier, *Community and Growth*, 25.
25   J. Vanier, *The Heart of L'Arche*, 62.

Out of the Depths:
Knowing God in Mental Illness

NOREEN MURRAY DMJ

The graced moment of encounter with love at the heart of suffering is the mystery I wish to explore. The particular context of the exploration is the experience of the suffering of mental illness. Its foundation stone is the belief that God, or however we wish to name ultimate reality, is revealed as intimate personal presence even in the darkest places. The starting point for Christian faith is the Resurrection of Jesus Christ. If Christ is risen that means that Light penetrates the deepest darkness. The graced moment of encounter with love experienced at the limit of darkness is resurrection. 'Out of the depths,' we are invited to wake up and find ourselves held gently in Love's embrace.

This essay is born of a life-long reflection and search for an understanding of the meaning of suffering. In my late teens I suffered a depression which lasted for nine months. At that time I did not have the label 'depression' to describe the experience. I truly did not know what was happening to me. I went to bed fearful of the night and rose in the morning dreading the day. Thinking that this was a unique experience, I lived in the bleakest darkness without any hope. Nearly forty years later I can still recall the first infinitesimal speck of light appearing at the end of a tunnel, a speck that proved to be real, and which grew slowly until I emerged into joy. Nine months gestation for the birth of joy! I have experienced dark times since then, but never as dark because no matter how terrible things seem the remembrance of the dawning light as something undeniably real sustains me and I fall through the dark into joy. But even joy is shot through with pain as I carry an awareness of the suffering of the world and stand a witness to the despair of those close to me.

A cradle Catholic, my journey started and continues within the perimeters of Christianity, particularly contemplating the mystery of the passion, death and resurrection of Jesus. Psychology made a formal entrance on to the stage of my life in the late sixties when, as a student nurse, I was introduced to the theory of defence mechanism. A window opened in my mind and I caught a glimpse of my defended nature.

Thus began a search for self-understanding, which is as enduring as the pondering of the mystery of Jesus, a search that is always set in the midst of a wider context of connectedness to all suffering. Unfortunately the spiritual quest and the quest for psychological understanding were often set over and against each other particularly by the suggestion that the pursuit of a spiritual path was simply, and only, a denial of the human origins and internal dynamics of a conflicted nature. The recognition that some God images did indeed serve that function only compounded the confusion, which effected a deep split inside that set spirituality and psychology in opposing camps while I struggled not to deny the validity of either. In this I believe I am a child of my times. Exploring issues of suffering in a theological context I was sometimes troubled by the stated reluctance 'to go down the path of psychopathology,' and I wondered who then would go there? God must be found there too.

I believe that the alienation of the spiritual in psychiatry has contributed to loss of hope, a distinctive aspect of the suffering of those with mental illness. The essay then had a two-pronged aim: to probe whether the encounter between helper and client is a locus for encounter with the Risen Lord and to explore the transforming power of Love. The discussion is based on nine in-depth interviews. Issues were explored from three different perspectives, service users, chaplains, and other professionals, in order to gain a more complete view.

Transcendence

Transcendence implies experience and appreciation of a dimension beyond the self that opens into Absolute Mystery. The capacity for transcendence inherent in the gift of our humanity must take account of another reality, the fact that the human person is created free. Stephen Duffy notes grace in freedom. Human beings, he says, 'are so structured that should they freely accept and open themselves to their dynamic intentionality and its transcendent horizon, they already render themselves affirmatively related to the God who reveals Godself, even though the reality of revelation and grace is not called by those names, or is, perhaps rejected.'[1]

An offer is made which must be accepted freely. Leonardo Boff's use of the word 'passion' in the context of openness to the transcendent captures a depth of human longing, of human desire. He says: 'human beings exist as a living transcendence, ever open and beyond themselves, ever moved by a passion for the infinite.'[2] Desire presents us with a choice: we can kill it choosing a living death or ultimately suicide, or we can engage our desire in a life quest for that which can satisfy.

The starting point of our quest for meaning requires that we stop running away and turn towards our desires in order to experience them deeply. We need to hold the tension and pain inherent in deep listening to our yearnings and we need to give them expression. Attending to our desires we bring to awareness our thirst for an understanding that will make sense of and give purpose and meaning to our lives. This turning towards our desire constitutes an opening to transcendence, a breach in the wall of self-enclosure. In the Christian revelation the cross of Jesus stands in the breach, there the limit of darkness is experienced and overcome in the death and resurrection of Jesus. In front of the cross, fully facing the chaos, we may find ourselves accepted at our worst, and discover our deepest reality brought to life by the dynamic power of love.

The Forgotten Dimension

An appreciation of transcendence was found to be of significance to all the participants in the interviews. Service users all referred specifically to belief in God as an important factor in their daily lives. God was seen as support in time of need and prayers were offered in thanksgiving for assistance received and for help to keep going. The belief was held that God would look after all the brokenness. Awakening to spirituality and discovering a personal relationship with Jesus Christ was for one person the most significant healing factor in life, loosening the control of the illness, bringing them into reality and making them content and happier.

Values were seen as part and parcel of spirituality. The primary value was respect for the personhood of the individual. To look on the person as a unique individual and to accept the person totally in all their human reality, of which their illness is just one factor, was paramount. The question was asked, do you see the service-user as a human being or as a condition? An emphasis on patience, listening, presence, attentiveness, compassion, empathy, all flowed from the primary value of the service-user as human being. The outcome of such attitudes led to relationships based on common humanity and relationships of equality. Such relationships enable responsibility, which can be a first stepping-stone on a pathway to integration. The relentless expression of the desire to be treated as persons and the profound sense of gratitude to those who thus treat them witnessed, sadly, to the rarity of this occurrence in the lives of service-users.

Placing the value of the person as a unique individual at the centre of service leads to programmes being devised which are designed to be person-centred and needs driven, tailor-made to meet the needs of the unique person. The interviewees mentioned many programmes that are in place to meet such needs. These include vocational, social, rehabilitation, counselling, information services, natural development, employment, creative work groups, health support, guidance, art, tai chi, and yoga.

A lacuna in these programmes seemed to be an attention to the spiritual needs of the person. One has to ask why is this aspect of need in the person excluded? The fear of being directive, expressed by one professional, is not a satisfactory reason. Why is one not afraid of being directive in all other areas of a person's life? This lacuna highlights the point that spirituality is as John Swinton asserts 'the forgotten dimension' within the contemporary practice of mental health care.[3] Psychiatrist Michael Corry and psychotherapist Áine Tubridy, living in Ireland, observed in their practice that the traditional approach to mental illness was patently not working. They felt they were cooking the books by ignoring this reality, and were forced by what they were witnessing to go in search for answers elsewhere. It became impossible for them to ignore the spiritual dimension.[4] They stand now with Swinton, and others who are engaged in developing a new paradigm of mental health care that includes the spiritual dimension as a significant aspect.

Suffering
Suffering is life's deepest mystery. Suffering in mental illness is a horrific experience impossible to describe. It is terrifying, tormenting, maddening, emotionally crushing, confusing, disturbing. One feels in

bits, over the edge, a prisoner of one's own mind, full of rage and self hatred, restless, agitated, isolated, lonely, forgotten, of no value. The image of the abyss powerfully symbolises the terrifying black pit of meaninglessness into which a person slides during the experience of mental illness. It is a meaningless void within which strength, hope and light are drained. The person is left stranded in a dark and lonely place where hope and possibility are banished and replaced with questions for which there appear to be no answers.

Fear is the climate in which mental illness is lived out. The sufferer is afraid: one participant said, the greatest pain is fear of what is happening. Fear and shock are very difficult to discuss as they propel the person into silence. Not only is the sufferer afraid, the onlookers are also afraid. The onlookers are so afraid that the only way they find to cope is by using the powerful and cruel weapon of avoidance, thus creating stigma. This means that on top of fears that arise from within, people with a mental illness find themselves ridiculed and alienated from without. This compounds their suffering and contributes to feelings of insecurity and a sense of being of no value, of being non-persons and to the loss of relationship in community. It can be no surprise then that the emotions of rage and terror also surface.

Of what is it that everybody is afraid? That is the question that most people seek to avoid and which, as Walter Mindell points out, the phenomenon of mental illness in society may be asking us to confront. Reflecting on his meetings with people suffering from schizophrenia, Mindell suggests that through the person suffering from mental illness, the collective unconscious is trying to express itself or show how the universe is evolving, in such a way as to make us more aware of the meaning of life. He points out that the encounter with mental illness can inform the general public about its conflicts and press society to formulate theories and think about issues that we would otherwise neglect.[5] Along the same lines Anne and Barry Ulanov state: 'The neurotic is the weak link in the chain of humanity. His very permeability makes him a living transmitter of what is almost always missing in collective conscious adaptation – unconscious life. The neurotic offers a channel through which unconscious contents can enter collective consciousness. For the neurotic stands out from the host of people who need this missing piece as much as he does by his own obsessive, compelling need to find it. He knows he cannot survive without it. His conscious plight, his loud suffering despair, amplifies the sound of need, which others only murmur."[6]

It is easier to scapegoat, to exclude, to allow others to carry the shadow, than it is to engage in personal soul searching or cultural critique which necessitates a confrontation with fears, biases and taboos, which threaten and might ultimately demand a change in values and behaviour of a society that is itself sick, deviant and in need of help. One of the mechanisms used to flee from those perceived as afflicted is to dehumanise them. This operates through the 'them and us' fiction that hides the reasons for society's need to scapegoat wounded people. The process of dehumanisation is very subtle, but when revealed, frightening in its depth and intensity. According to T. Kitwood, 'a consensus is created, established in tradition and embedded in social practices, that those affected are not real persons.'[7] And as Swinton says, 'people become identified by their pathologies ... terms that substitute their primary identity as human beings made in God's image and passionately loved by God, for a socially constructed way of being that seriously limits their life possibilities. Socially deprived of identity, they are forced to adopt images and roles that strip them of many of the basics of acceptable human living.'[8]

On the spiritual level their experience is often discarded as nothing but the product of their illness and consequently relegated to the realm of symptomatology rather than respected as meaningful human experience. To dehumanise others is to oppress them, using power to prevent a person from becoming fully human and thus fully reflective of the image of God.

Such forces of oppression are active in Ireland today. Amnesty International's February 2003 report, 'Mental Illness, the Neglected Quarter' reveals that Irish mental health care services fail to comply fully with international human rights. Even though one in four people are affected by mental illness, mental health has never had priority for Irish governments. Government inaction is due in large part to a failure of public opinion to galvanise politicians sufficiently to put the necessary resources into mental health care. According to Amnesty the huge stigma shrouding mental illness in Ireland stems from a lack of public understanding about the issue. Among its recommendations it urges the government to implement a public education and awareness campaign to counter the stigma of mental illness.

As welcome as such moves are, one has to wonder if such an approach can go deep enough to enable people to face up to the reality that of stigmatisation helps to keep at bay, and to encourage a search for deeper understandings of the meaning of mental suffering. People seeking together an understanding of the phenomenon of mental illness, and the most effective ways of relating to it, may lead to a deeper understandings of the meaning of many kinds of suffering, an understanding which may bear witness to the possibility of transforming the vast spectrum of pain into wisdom, compassion and the art of living a fully human life.

Community

The primary desire identified in the conversations was respect for the personhood of the individual leading to relationships based on common humanity, relationships of equality such are as the heart of genuine community. The Church is a community, which mirrors the mystery of love in the Trinity. In the Christian revelation God is revealed as a mystery of love among three persons. This means that every human being has his or her origin in a person who by definition is not solitary but is called to relationship with another: The human then is also by definition 'a being in relationship'. As Olivier Clements says: 'What could be called the 'Trinitarian person' is not the isolated individual of Western society ... Nor is it the absorbed and amalgamated human being of totalitarian society, or of systematised oriental mysticism, or of the sects. It is, and must be, a person in a relationship, in communion.'[9] Communion means shared life. Persons who exist together in true communion share happiness, share hope, share suffering, share responsibility. In such a community each person is unique, no one person is more important than another is.

The Church, as a community that mirrors this mystery of love among the three persons of the Trinity, is sadly not reflected in the services to mental illness. While some participants find a source of inspiration and nourishment in Liturgy, their experience of Church community is a negative one. Participants lamented the lack of a welcoming community.

Experience in Church is contrasted with experience in some secular communities. There they find values of community, which perhaps should be the identifying characteristics of a true Christian community; welcome, acceptance, sharing, support, and caring. In contrast they reported a sad lack of understanding by parish communities. A welcoming hand is not extended to people with mental illness, in contrast to the efforts made to welcome and facilitate other groups such as people with learning disability. The reality is that people with mental health problems feel that isolation and abandonment by everybody.

Perhaps it is a scandal that they experience the church community, in the parish, as a place of rejection. It was noted that Church and society are often identical in terms of attitude and response to those with a mental illness rather than the Church exercising prophetic leadership.

One participant commented that if the Church were Church it would be breaking ground, the leaders of the Church would be preaching but they are not. This did not surprise this participant because he saw the Church as simply a congregation of people, who often reflect the values of the society in which they are immersed. If the society excludes the mentally ill then the Church congregation will so exclude. Perhaps this view of an outsider highlights the loss, in the field of mental illness, of the prophetic role of the Church.

Historical reasons are relevant to an understanding of contemporary non-acceptance in Irish society of the reality of mental illness in its midst. Historically mental illness was hidden away behind the closed doors of large institutions. It was pointed out in the conversations that it is only sixteen years since the community-based programmes came into being. 'We are still only in our infancy, we are still embryonic, we have much to learn.' 'It's a new thing, there is not the same established communication as there is with other disabilities.'

Regarding a multidisciplinary approach to services, it was found that those services whose ethos arises from a history in Religious Congregations include chaplains in their multidisciplinary teams. Other services do not. In the latter chaplains are respected, but are not integral to the service. Even in those services, which give a role to chaplains, the numbers of chaplains employed tells its own story. One chaplain may have the responsibility for an institution and all the community outreach services, including hostels, in a Health Board area.

To the Future

Future research could address the question posed by one professional participant. He asked: 'Is there a methodology in which we could incorporate the spiritual aspect into our programme without doing any harm?' This question places the onus for coming up with suggestions on those whose primary purpose is spiritual ministry. The question indicates an openness to dialogue. There is a body of knowledge already available in the experience of chaplains engaged in full time ministry, which could be tapped into to help devise a programme that would be acceptable and workable for those services whose ethos does not facilitate the incorporation of the spiritual dimension as integral to their programme of service to those suffering from mental illness.

A practical response could be a parish-based survey, which would seek to identify forms of outreach to those who suffer from mental illness in their midst. But such an exploration cannot succeed, it seems to me, without a concurrent programme of parish-based spiritual formation. This formation will set people on a spiritual path, a path which is not a way of avoidance, but a journey which will enable people to face that which we all tend to ignore, to postpone or to evade; the pervasive and often nameless fear that rules our lives, what one service user named as the, 'deep seated repressed fear of who we are.' Fear experienced as threat is the everyday face of death. Acknowledging our fears allows us to be in solidarity with all human weakness. The ultimate in human suffering is the Godforsakeness experienced by Jesus on the cross of Calvary. All suffering is gathered into the suffering of Jesus. A spiritual path that resolutely faces into dark mystery, is a journey in the footsteps of Jesus Christ who leads the way into death and through death to new life. To be baptised is to die and rise again with Christ. 'To die to the death that is so deeply entwined with our life. To cry out *de profundis* and to meet even in hell the crucified God who does not judge, but welcomes us and who, in return for the least good will on our part ... raises us to life with himself.'[10] To offer anything less than a journey through death into new life is to deny the reality of the baptism by which we have entered into the community of the Church.

The conversations highlighted that the plight of those who are suffering from mental illness is of a very serious nature and the proposal, the spiritual dimension is un addressed. That is not too surprising. What was surprising was the extent of the alienation of those suffering from mental illness from the Church community. Thus, the spiritual dimension of the person suffering from mental illness is lost between two stools, psychiatry and the Church. The need to bring the spiritual dimension from the periphery to the centre of psychiatry fades into insignificance when compared with the need to bring the person with mental illness to the centre of the Church so that a fragile hope can be fanned into life. Mary Barnes account of her journey through madness kindled the hope that mental torment may yield to personal redemption. In her poem 'Cud of my Soul'[11] Love invites all those with mental illness to:

Creep near,
before the Fire of my love
and violent as the Flame of Truth
shall I clutch the glowing embers of your souls,
and from you shall burn a fire so brilliant, so piercing,
that all may know that I,
the Lord your God,
brought you here;
to your own lives.

Writing on the cover of Mary's book, *Something Sacred*, Dr J. Berke said that her life demonstrates the sustained transformation of a raw, despairing, regressed former patient into an artist, a helper, a healer, and most profoundly, a supple soul.

The experience of being respected and accepted in their whole reality, part of which is the reality of mental illness, is the relational catalyst which enables the possibility of transformation in a graced encounter with Love.

Notes

1   S. J. Duffy, *The Graced Horizon* (Minnesota: The Liturgical Press, 1992) 236.

2   L. Boff, *Liberating Grace* (New York: Orbis Books, 1988) 179.

3   J. Swinton, *Spirituality and Mental Health Care* (London: Jessica Kingsley, 2001) 8.

4   M. Corry & Á. Tubridy, *Going Mad?* (Dublin: New Leaf, 2001) ix-xi.

5   W. Mindell, *City Shadows* (London: Arkana, 1991) 162-168.

6   A. & B. Ulanov, *Religion and the Unconscious* (Philadelphia, The Westminster Press, 1995) 193.

7   T. Kitwood, *Dementia Reconsidered: The Person Comes First* (Orlando: Open University Press, 1997) 12.

8   J. Swinton, *Resurrecting the Person* (Abingdon Press, 2000) 10

9   O. Clements, *The Roots of Christian Mysticism* (London: New City, 1993) 65-66.

10   Ibid.

11   M. Barnes with A. Scott, *Something Sacred* (London: Free Association Books, 1989) 138. In 1966 Mary Barnes was a schizophrenic with no hope of relief from her condition and Joseph Berke was a young doctor in rebellion against the restrictions of the American psychiatric profession. Berke moved to England to work with R.D. Laing. There he met Mary as a patient.

Performing God: Presenting Scripture Through Theatre

JOE KILLICK

'And the word was made flesh ...' – this statement is, perhaps, most evidently true when it comes to a dramatic theatrical performance. A group of performers gather to present, in real time, real characters to another group or community, i.e. the audience. In other words, the written word is made alive or incarnated. Flesh and bones are grafted onto the text, adding the missing non-verbal levels of communication that living beings convey to each other.

If the performing arts are used to present Scripture, does the Word become more alive and relevant to a contemporary audience and does it help to enhance the spirituality of those involved – the presenters and the audience? These are the main questions this article will briefly seek to address.

Our discussion will focus on a short exploration of the nature of the performing arts, such as drama, dance and music. We will also discuss the relationship between art and the divine and will seek to show how the arts can be a means of meeting our innate desire for God. We will also explore how the 'felt' experience or non-rational knowing in art can be related to, or is analogous with, the experience of the 'Holy'. In more practical terms we will look at the results of qualitative research that was carried out with the Slightly Brilliant Theatre Company (SBTC), an amateur theatrical company based in All Hallows College, Dublin. SBTC is a Christian organisation established to encourage people into a deeper relationship with God, which has always been the challenge facing anyone engaged in communicating the Christian message.

Act One: The Performing Arts

Because of the near permanent form in which they exist, paintings, sculpture and the written form of literature and music, can be studied over time. In this way their artistic and aesthetic qualities can be assessed and appreciated. But what of the less permanent nature of theatrical performance, the performance of drama, music, mime, dance, ballet, opera, considered separately or in various combinations? Does their performance qualify as 'art'? While the question of what constitutes 'art' is far too broad to cover here, nonetheless it is useful in the context of this article to consider what is meant by the performing arts.

Drama and music are recognised as art forms, but quite often this has meant the permanent form of the text, that is, the script and the score, rather than the performance of the text. While today it is possible to study the recorded performance on film, CD, DVD, video or tape, no matter how well produced, they all lack the quality or special nature of the live event.

It is the immediacy of the live theatrical performance that makes it special as an art form. It must also be said, however, that it is its very immediacy, its ephemerality, that creates a difficulty in studying its aesthetic qualities. Yet performance was in existence long before the permanency of text came into being; the performing arts are by their very nature temporal. Each performance of the same text differs because of the vicissitudes of being that is the life of the human, particularly that of the performers, but including the audience who are an integral part of the theatrical experience.

Just because a work appeals to the senses, and thus gives pleasure, does not necessarily mean that it exists or is performed for aesthetic reasons. Theatrical performances have often, over many centuries, been regarded as crude, lewd and popular forms of entertainment with few aesthetic or moral qualities. It has, and continues to have, exponents who use it in this manner merely to make money through cheap laughs and sexual excitement. If this is the intention then clearly it is not a work of art, even if inadvertently such a work contains elements of the aesthetic, because as Frank Burch Brown in *Religious Aesthetics* points out 'an artwork is something produced with the intention of giving it the capacity to satisfy the aesthetic interest'. Providing this is the intention of the creators, performance can provide 'aesthetic delight.' [1]

However, this criterion on its own would not qualify performance as an art form. A work of art must not only appeal to the senses, it must also be imaginatively, skillfully and knowledgeably made. Most works of art, except perhaps architecture, have no utilitarian purpose other than to provide aesthetic delight, and also 'might be beautiful, expressive, representational, or prophetic'[2].

The rehearsal process

There can be no denying that performance is, at its highest level, brought about by inspired, skilful and knowledgeable making. It is born out of the imagination and through careful rehearsal brought to life. During this process the performers use many skills so as to incarnate a fictional character and portray this other self to others in performance. They have to become aware of their own bodies, minds and emotions. Theatre, and in particular drama, has been recognised traditionally as a valuable means of teaching self-awareness. In education, drama is used as a way for children and adults to experience a situation or to walk in the shoes of another person. Rather than feeding the mind with information, the student embodies the person and explores a situation using his or her whole self. Performers in rehearsal and training learn to use their whole selves (body, mind and spirit) as powerful instruments of communication. They develop their vocal, movement, imaginative and memory skills, as well as their emotional and feeling awareness in order to improve their powers of expression.

Either explicitly or implicitly, the performer gains a vital understanding of the complexity of how human beings communicate. In training and rehearsal the actor, singer and dancer learn that it is not just the verbal that is a vital element in human expression and communication, but also the non-verbal. Body language, gesture, and facial expression add flesh to the words and act as signposts or signals to the deeper and nuanced layers of meaning of characters and stories. These signals are often very subtle, but are perceived by the observer – in this case, the audience. They read the truth of the performance from these signals and consciously or unconsciously choose to believe or not to believe in its reality. A skill performers have to learn is that of concentrating on remaining in the present moment of the virtual reality they seek to create.

During the creative process of rehearsal the performer uses the power of imagination to bring alive the fictional character or idea in the act of incarnation. It is often through the power of imaginative inspiration that heights of aesthetic and artistic expression, meaning and truth are achieved and communicated to others.

Performance as a Mode of Communication and a Method of Teaching
The theatre has long been recognised as a means of communicating information, a method of transmitting a message. It is a powerful medium, which can be used for good or evil. Its power to influence is well attested to by the censorious attitude it has encountered over the centuries from Church and state, even though both were not averse to using its power when it was convenient. Because the theatre is the art of the here and now, it presents fictional characters as real. The audience is willing, for the duration of the performance at least, to suspend its disbelief and accept them as such. And this is precisely why many philosophers and theologians saw a great danger in theatrical performance. It seems there always has been the contention that the performers and the audience would begin to believe the reality of the fiction presented to them and that their morals would be adversely affected. Not all philosophers shared these opinions. Aristotle defended theatre on the grounds that in presenting evil it was effectively disarmed. He believed that by presenting the grosser desires and emotions artistically the audience could purge themselves of them through catharsis.

From their earliest days the Jesuits were very aware of the didactic benefits of theatre, which they employed through performances of the mystery and miracle plays. William H. McCabe in *An Introduction to Jesuit Theatre* describes how they used the theatre to 'improve the morals of men ... Comedy's purpose is chiefly to instruct common people by examples that are close to home, taken from ordinary life; but tragedy is designed to instruct princes and men of high estate.' [3] This obviously only applied to the male of the species. Women, apparently, were deemed not to need instruction as they were not even allowed into the theatre!

The Jesuits used all forms of theatre, that is, 'comedy, tragedy, the ballet ("painting in motion"), and the opera ("poetry that sings"), ...as useful and agreeable instructions'. [4] It is perhaps the pleasure it gives to a number of senses simultaneously that makes theatre such a "dangerous" medium, because we tend to learn and absorb quicker that which is presented through pleasure. Modern television advertising methods attest to this notion.

The pleasure of storytelling has been part of humankind's make-up since we began to communicate with one another. We have always loved to gather in community and share stories, whether it is around the campfire or in the auditorium of a theatre. Human beings seem to have a natural instinct for imitation and an inbuilt feeling for music and rhythm.

In pre-literate times our initial attempts at communication were through imitation, using crude sounds and movements. Over time these crude sounds and movements developed into rhythmical dances and music and these then became an accepted method of passing on a people's history and a way of informing and teaching the following generations. Movement and rhythm are fundamental to how we communicate, and to life. Without movement we would die. Our hearts, the organ of life, beat in a certain rhythm, which Jean-Louis Barrault described as the short and long beat of the 'iamb ... the fundamental rhythm of poetry'.[5]

As we developed our powers of communication we became aware of the power of rhythm and movement to express and communicate the ineffable, a way of gaining access to the unconscious. Rhythm and movement are the essential elements of art. Through their conscious use they allow artists to achieve the classic aesthetic elements of harmony, balance and proportion in their work, and to communicate an understanding of that which is the transcendent part of life. In the performing arts, their use appeals immediately to a variety of senses at the same time.

But what is performance? Performance happens when a person or a group of people, the performers, work (rehearse) to present a story in a space using the elements of theatre and when a group of people, the audience, agree to actively participate by attending this presentation. There is an intimacy created when these two groups meet, a mutual sharing of a living experience. It is through the rhythm of the spoken word, music, singing, dancing, colour in the lighting, costumes and setting, the live immediate intimacy, and the interactive participation of performers and audience, that the art of performance is imbued with its power to educate and communicate. And because theatre uses the human body moving in space as its medium, it is in and through the body that something of the transcendent part of our human nature is mediated and incarnated. The art of theatre has the possibility of bringing those who experience it to the liminal space between the ordinary and the transcendent. It can offer an opportunity of entering the doorway to the Holy.

Act 2: Art: A Doorway to the Holy?
Individuals today, as in the past, are seeking meaning, depth and truth in their lives from a variety of sources outside organised or mainstream

religions. This is manifest in the growth of the New Age Movement and the popular psychology industry. People have a desire for the more of life, the transcendent, the spiritual. In a Christian sense, this desire can be interpreted, to paraphrase Augustine, as the desire to rest in God, the desire for the experience of the transcendent. How we strive to meet this desire for the sacred, the holy, is our spirituality. The arts can be a means of assisting our striving to satisfy this desire for God.

Traditionally, Western Christian theology has been predominantly concerned with the understanding of God through conceptual and rational terms. It could be said to have failed to admit the possibility of coming to "know" God in non-rational terms, except for the Church Fathers of early Christianity, and in mystical theology. Rational thought and concepts are vital in our attempts to come to an understanding of God, but a purely verbally based theology without a non-verbal, non-rational factor, is an impoverished one. To ignore the fact that God can be experienced or apprehended in a sensible way through a "feeling" about something outside the person, would be to present what Rudolf Otto calls a 'one-sidedly intellectualistic and rationalistic interpretation'[6] of the idea God. A profound experience of the sacred, or the Holy, evokes feeling responses in the person that are partly ineffable or inexpressible. These 'creature-feelings' are a reflection or a shadow of deeper feelings evoked by the felt presence of the numinous, something that is related to, or characteristic of, the divine.[7] All human beings have deep within them a non-rational awareness of that which we call God and it is through the arts, amongst other phenomena, that it may be experienced and perhaps partially expressed.

Experience of the Holy in the arts

All true artists strive to express that which is deep within the human person, be it called truth, goodness, beauty or meaning of life. While many might not refer to it as such, they try to bring to expression that sense of the numinous that is within. A genuine work of art has the capability to evoke in its observer feelings of awareness that are analogous to the awareness of the Holy that is innate in everyone.

According to Otto the sublime in the arts is 'the most effective means of expressing the numinous'[8] and through this sublime element they evoke within us a sense of the *mysterium tremendum et fascinans,* the 'awe-ful' and fascinating mystery. This sense of tremendous wonder is something beyond what may be termed ordinary wonder and is difficult to express to others. Our everyday ordinary language seems quite inadequate to describe such profound moments. Many mystics have over the centuries attempted to convey something of this encounter with the Holy and artists struggle to communicate a sense of it through poetry, literature, music, the visual arts, drama, dance and architecture.

It is often perceived that such an experience is beyond the ordinary mortal, but it may be more evident than we might suppose. For instance, how many of us have experienced such a moment when we, on seeing something really beautiful, a sunset or an exquisite work of art, have been lifted out of ourselves and when everything around us seems to be seen and experienced in a clear light of non-rational knowing? At this precise moment time seems to stand still and we seem to be at-one with everything. We are caught up in a moment of profound awareness of mystery, awesomeness and a sense of one's 'littleness' in the face of something wondrous and magnificent that is beyond oneself. In this instant our normal intellectual and emotional responses are suspended.

The moment we become aware of our reactions we come out of the experience and back to our own reality. Then, initially, we may be affected emotionally by the sheer beauty, or sublimity, of the moment. If it was a work of art that evoked such a moment, we may begin to rationally appraise the object and begin to appreciate it simply for its own sake, as a monument to human endeavour; a celebration of the artistry, skill and craft of those involved in the design and construction. In other words, we appreciate it purely as an object of aesthetic delight.

But for a religiously orientated person, this moment of awe and wonder can be viewed from another perspective. It would be experienced as an encounter with the numinous, reminding one of the glory of God, and also of a sense of God's immanence. And thus the beauty of the work of art was conveying something of the divine and capable of evoking a personal religious experience. Its beauty would be seen as a reflection of the ultimate Beauty that is God.

But is it, therefore, only at the higher levels of refined appreciation and execution of the arts that there exists such a possibility of evoking a religious experience? This would surely alienate and exclude many who intentionally strive to create or participate in something meaningful, say, a liturgical drama or movement, even though the execution of it may not reach any great heights of artistic or aesthetic accomplishment. Does this mean then that the possibility of a relationship with God through these circumstances is diminished or even non-existent?

In attending and participating in such liturgies, no matter how well, or badly, presented, people are seeking to create an aspect of beauty. They are seeking an experience of the divine, to experience something of the mystery that words alone cannot achieve.

The Transcendent in Art

The role of art is to get behind and/or question the perceptions of reality of everyday existence. Art has the task, as Langdon B. Gilkey says, of exposing 'the truth behind and within the ordinary'[9]. When the ordinary is portrayed artistically it is heightened and richly endowed with symbol and meaning. In a theatrical performance the seemingly ordinary has significance greater than it normally would. On a micro level, a gesture or a look communicates more significance because it is under greater scrutiny by the onlooker and because the actor has rehearsed it and enacts it precisely to convey enhanced meaning. On the macro level, the theatrical performance as a whole seeks to convey greater significance and meaning through a heightened experience of the whole. If during this heightened experience all elements converge to create a moment of 'intense seeing', a moment of sheer beauty, a moment of unification in which time seems to stand still, then the 'transcendent appears through art, and art and religion approach one another'[10]. In the theatre, when all the parts gel, there is what is termed in the business, 'a moment of theatre'. It is a 'magical' moment that is experienced by the community of audience and cast alike. It is a meeting of minds and hearts, a shared moment of beauty in which all are aware of something beyond the ordinary, a palpable something understood by everyone, or most, at least; something that is greater than the sum of the parts that conveys meaning and a sense of truth and beauty. This enhanced experience may touch the recipient in a deep way and may raise the mind to considerations of the transcendent dimension of being. It may evoke within the individual a personal religious experience.

A genuine religious experience in the sense of direct contact with the divine is impossible. Even the most profound visions and experiences of God are, and always will be, experienced by human beings as 'a dim reflection in a mirror'. (1 Cor 13:12). All that art can do in the religious sense is create a doorway to a religious experience, which raises the senses and the mind to a dim reflection of the holy, a heightened awareness of God's presence in the world. If participation in the arts, and in particular, the theatre, can thus draw the participant, either as performer or on-looker, into a deeper or enhanced relationship with God, then it can be seen as being spiritual and as having a spirituality.

Act 3: Models of Spirituality

What is spirituality? Is it all things to all people? Many books and articles on spirituality begin their discussion by acknowledging that it is a word that is used quite freely and to which there are many meanings. As a consequence, it is often very difficult to know precisely what is meant by spirituality. In the context of this article, spirituality is defined as a way of being that strives for a relationship with the transcendent or mysterious spirit. It is our lived experience of God, either personally or in a communal sense, and it is concerned with the totality of the person.

How we act or strive to satisfy our fundamental desire for the transcendent is our spirituality. It is our way of being in the world. While some manifest this way of being in a destructive manner by seeking relief through self-centredness, drink, drugs or other forms of self-gratification, many others strive, consciously or unconsciously, for self-transcendence through loving relationships, religious or spiritual paths and through art.

As was illustrated above, the arts have the capability of evoking a religious, or a spiritual, experience in those engaged in and with them. True art seeks to find an expression of meaning and truth. To participate in the arts is therefore a way of being that strives for a relationship with the transcendent mystery of the divine. As John Paul II states in his *Letter to Artists*:

> Every genuine art form in its own way is a path to the inmost reality of man and of the world.[11]

The theatre is one such path and also a unique art form insofar as it can make use of the artistry of the poet, writer, sculptor, architect, musician, actor. But what of its spirituality? How does one assess this in the light of so many different disciplines? Two main areas or levels of assessment present themselves: that of the organisation presenting a performance and that of the individuals involved in the presentation. By applying models of spirituality to these two spheres, an evaluation of the spiritualities may be made.

However, in order to consider models of spirituality against which to make an evaluation of the spirituality of presenting Scripture in a theatrical format, it is necessary to clarify what is meant by such terms as religious experience, spiritual experience and experience of the divine or of God, which may be constituent parts of any spirituality.

Bernadette Flanagan, in her book *The Spirit of the City,* gives a useful breakdown of the distinctions between these terms.[12] *Religious experience* may be defined as an acute awareness of some 'power or presence' that is beyond our everyday awareness. It is not something that is present on an on-going basis but is experienced as something ephemeral. As we have seen, art may be experienced in this way.

In contrast, *spiritual experience* may be considered as being more mindfully engaged with 'issues of growth rather than [being] confined to ... incidental moments of depth'. Spiritual experience in this case is understood to be concerned with the development of the whole person. Again, art, and in particular theatre, can play a vital role in this development.

Another aspect of spirituality is that of the *experience of God*. It is the desire for an encounter with God or, to put it in Ignatian terms, the desire to find God in all things. Prayer, and possibly reflection, would be characteristic of this form of spirituality involving as it does an active search for an experience of God in our everyday lives.

A model of spirituality based on the above premises, which, of course, are often overlapping and not clear-cut separate spheres, may be characterised as a holistic developmental or growth model, as it is concerned with the development of the whole person – body, mind and spirit.

One of the main aims of the Slightly Brilliant Theatre Company (SBTC) the research field, is to help the individual develop intellectually, humanly, professionally, vocationally and spiritually, in other words, to help the individual discover her or his true self. Therefore, the holistic developmental model of spirituality described above would appear to be appropriate.

However, because we are dealing not just with the individual in isolation, but with community, it is also appropriate to consider community-oriented spiritualities. The theatre by its very nature is communal. There is the community of the company itself, and there is the broader community formed by the company and the audience on the occasions of performance. Hans-Georg Gadamer, in *The Relevance of the Beautiful*, refers to the theatre as being an 'immediate communal experience' in which a 'vital interchange' takes place between 'player and onlooker'[13]. This experience is of a spiritual, transformative nature that awakens us to 'new possibilities of being that go beyond what we are'[14].

In a community model of spirituality, the concern is one of outreach. In other words: Does the organisation have an ethos or policy of reaching out or communicating with others outside of itself? Does it seek to provide for its players and onlookers an experience that has the possibility of taking us beyond ourselves and creating a kind of transformed reality?

The SBTC seeks to daringly present contemporary issues in the context of the Scriptures through 'bold experiments' and there is also a strong emphasis on an international dimension in the group so that those in the group, and the audiences, can experience other cultures.

Two other models of spirituality that deserve consideration in our context of theatre and spirituality are derived from *kataphatic* and *apophatic* approaches in theology.

In the first approach, the kataphatic, the content of religious or spiritual experience is important. This could be described as the seeking of God's presence in all things: in nature, art, life experiences and so on. Gerald G. May calls this approach 'content-oriented'.[15]

In opposition to this model is what May describes as 'consciousness-oriented' or apophatic spirituality[15]. The main characteristic of this approach is its focus on the mystical or mysterious reality of the divine. It is generally seen as opposing the use of any form of conceptual, precise language or imagery for "capturing" God, which some 'proponents feel ... constitutes idolatry'.[16]

Theatre may be seen by many as falling within the first category, that of the kataphatic. However, it is useful to remind ourselves that one approach does not necessarily rule out the presence of another. In fact, the argument put forward here is that the kataphatic elements of the theatre enhance or facilitate movement towards the apophatic, the mysterious reality of the divine.

By using the above models of spirituality as criteria to evaluate the Slightly Brilliant Theatre Company, some notion or appreciation of the spirituality or spiritualities of presenting Scripture in theatrical format was made.

The Research Environment

The Slightly Brilliant Theatre Company (SBTC) is based in All Hallows College, Drumcondra, Dublin. It came into existence in 1999 'to help a group of mostly young students who are slightly brilliant in many different ways and who so need a context within which to express their lives, their talents and their spiritual convictions'.[17]

The Company was formed by its present producer James (Jay) Shanahan, a Vincentian priest and Director of Media Studies at All Hallows College, who saw a need to bring alive the academic material of theology and Bible studies for students and for potential audiences. He was also seeking to utilise the College Chapel space in a more creative way.

Encouraging people into a deeper relationship with God has always been the challenge facing anyone engaged in communicating the Christian message. In the light of this challenge, the SBTC was established with three main aims – to engender in its participants a greater self-confidence in communication, to develop the skills to work at an individual and a group level, and to portray biblical stories in an imaginative contemporary context.

Participants are involved at all levels of production so that they may explore their own talents and bring those talents to bear in a dynamic, creative and practical way in their chosen careers. The production values used in the presentation of scriptural themes incorporate in imaginative and innovative ways most, if not all, the elements of theatre such as music, song, drama, art, poetry, mime, movement, dance and modern information technology in the form of graphic imagery. Using all the various elements of theatre, four original productions have been mounted to date:

- *Child – A Life In Song* (1999) was based on the birth of Jesus and its relevance for our life's journey
- *Dreams Beyond Frontiers* (2001) portrayed how Jesus, in His life, death and resurrection, transcended the boundaries of His time and illustrated how the lives of heroes in our world from diverse cultures challenge us to do likewise
- *Flame* (2002) was based on St Paul and the early Christian communities
- *Dawning* was based on the creation story and the early patriarchs.

These productions have engaged a total of more than two hundred and fifty students and staff, many of whom had no previous experience of production. They have been involved in singing, dancing, drama, mime, movement, and diverse levels of production (script writing, song selection and writing, lighting, set design, hospitality and stage management).

Act 4: Evaluation of the Spirituality of the Slightly Brilliant Theatre Company

It is evident from the research data that there is a strong sense of a communal spirituality present amongst members of the Company interviewed. For some this manifested itself as a lived experience of the mystery that is God, while others compared it to a basic Christian community. There was also a desire in the Company to engage in a 'vital exchange' with the broader community of the audience. For some of the members being involved in the SBTC represented an active search for God in all things.

There is also a pronounced awareness of the transcendent or divine presence that most call God. This awareness was variously described as 'something greater than us', the Holy Spirit, 'energy', 'something else' and 'this relationship'. These descriptions could perhaps be summed up by the expression John Paul II in his *Letter to Artists* refers to as a 'divine spark' of artistic vocation.[18] Those involved in composing music or creating dance routines described what could be termed 'moments of depth' or religious experiences. From the data it is possible to discern a 'spirituality of artistic service'.

There is also evidence of the *kataphatic* and the *apophatic* models of spirituality at work, at least among the creative personnel within the Company. While working on the kataphatic elements of performance, i.e., the imagery, dances, experiences of an apophatic nature were reported, wherein a sense of an ineffable presence became apparent to the individual. This seems to affirm the premise postulated earlier that the kataphatic elements of the theatre enhance or facilitate movement towards the apophatic, the mysterious reality of the divine.

A supportable claim can be made that SBTC's presentations represent an opportunity for some to become aware of the sublime and thereby experience feelings analogous to the numinous. This evidence is represented in the statements that attest to some people being affected deeply by the 'powerful', 'moving' and 'uplifting' experience of the performances, which, for one individual, 'transported me back into the New Testament'.

However, what is not capable of being evaluated from the data is the depth or quality of these reactions.

The support, encouragement for self-expression and the opportunities offered, and observed in practice, for the development of the person as a whole, coupled with the above trends would strongly suggest that the holistic model of spirituality, one that is concerned with the development of the whole person – body, mind and spirit, would be an appropriate one to define the overall spirituality of the Slightly Brilliant Theatre Company.

Epilogue

The main question to which an answer was sought was how, or if, involvement in the presentation of Scripture affected the spirituality of the participants.

All the research participants expressed, in varying degrees, a sense of growth in their spirituality since they had become involved with the SBTC. This manifested itself in a communal sense, in the way they had moved from a self-interested motivation that existed for some when they joined to a community based one of mutual support and awareness of others. This change was recognised by the interviewees themselves and was also apparent to this researcher. From a personal development perspective, there is ample evidence to show a considerable growth took place in relation to confidence, and creative and communication skills. There was also a stated growth in awareness of relationship with God, a point that will be covered in more detail below.

Some of the factors that have contributed to this growth were identified as the desire of the leadership to create a community of trust and respect for the individual, and to establish an environment where it was safe for the individual to explore her or his potentiality and, hopefully, to discover at least part of his or her true self. The religious and spiritual convictions of the leaders were deemed important by many of the interviewees. The way that they lived out, by example, the Christian message of the Scriptures that was being presented artistically was also important.

In essence, what can be deduced from this is the importance of creating, what one person described as a basic Christian community, where the preached – or in this case the performed – message is also the lived reality.

A central focus in this article was the question whether the Word of God became more alive and relevant when presented artistically. But what exactly does "more alive" mean? The phrases that come to mind are 'meaningful for', 'relevant to', and 'experienced wholly by the recipient in a real sense'. The evidence from the research clearly affirms that presenting Scripture in a theatrical format, in other words through art, helped make it more real and meaningful for those who engaged with it in this manner. Many of the respondents in the research process are studying or have studied theology at some level and would have gained an intellectual or rational knowledge of Scripture. But from the testimonies it is clear, that for some, they came to a fuller understanding of the Word when they experienced it through the art of performance, in other words, by doing theology through art.

This correlates strongly with what theologians such as Rahner, Von Balthasar, Otto, Tillich and Gilkey maintain, that is, that a rational theology without the non-rational is an impoverished form of knowledge or understanding. For example, Rahner in his *Theological Investigations*, makes the point that 'theology must somehow be "mystagogical", that is, it should not merely speak about objects in abstract concepts, but it must encourage people *really to experience* that which is expressed in such concepts.'[17] (Italics added) Many other commentators on art and theology, such as Hederman, Burch Brown, Lane and Viladesau, also contend that this experiential understanding can be gained through the arts, especially, as Burch Brown puts it, 'those richly aesthetic arts that can bring [intellectual forms of theology] imaginatively to life.'[18] And, as our respondents amply demonstrated, what better art form to do this than the theatre, which, to slightly misquote Von Balthasar, can render 'the history of salvation visible and make it live.'[19]

Theatre takes that which has happened in history and presents it in the immediate. SBTC takes biblical stories and, through the creative imagination of the artists, contextualises them in contemporary situations. It presents them through real people, for real people, in real time and in real space, so that the historical becomes a real experience for those involved, both audience and performers. For this to be a genuine experience it must also be what Gadamer terms an 'immediate communal experience of what we are ... and the new possibilities of being that go beyond what we are'.[20] One interviewee alluded to such an experience when he describes how he was 'so close to the action' that he 'felt drawn into the story' and how the experience challenged him to reflect on his present spiritual commitment.

The type of experience many of the interviewees described in relation to their engagement with the performing arts may rightly be called religious or depth experiences, the experience of the transcendent mystery that is God. These experiences invited reflection and challenged the interviewees to make a transformative response, which from the evidence some did.

But was it the performing arts *per se* that evoked these experiences or is there some other explanation? Some of the interviewees referred to a perceived difference between a Scripture-oriented production and a so-called 'secular' one. They did not relate this difference so much to the aesthetic and artistic merits of SBTC's productions, but more to the religious content of the shows and the particular spiritual environment in which they are presented. Was it, therefore, merely the religious content of these presentations that evoked the religious experiences described by some members of the Company? According to Gesa Thiessen, in her comprehensive study of the relationship between theology and art *Theology and Modern Irish Art*, 'the spiritual, transcendent, or even specifically Christian dimension in art, felt and experienced by the recipient, is not – or at least is not necessarily – dependent on religious subject matter'. [21]

It is the opinion of this researcher, based on his observations, his experience of theatre over a number of years and the literature reviewed in the course of this work, that it is the level of performance, whether or not the performance can be deemed to be genuine art, that determines the possibility of evoking a religious experience or of confronting the 'numinous itself'. The 'powerful' and 'moving' experiences attested to by two of the interviewees were in relation to a particularly good performance by the actor playing St Paul. Because of his skill, and that of others, there were moments in this production that verged on the sublime, and that could rightly be called powerful, aesthetically delightful and quite artistically accomplished in many respects. It could be termed what Gilkey calls 'an event that we label art … containing a moment of new awareness or understanding, a moment of intense seeing and of participation in what is seen. [It is then that] the transcendent appears through art, and art and religion approach one another.' [22] This supports the notion, that the performing arts are indeed a 'doorway to the Holy'.

What has also emerged from the research is the perceived need to enliven the Liturgy. What seems to be missing is a sense of the mysterious, the sense of the 'wholly other' and this, interestingly, echoes sentiments made by Otto in 1917 about the Mass. [23] There is a case to be made for the greater, more creative, imaginative, and contextual use of the performing arts in modern Liturgy.

How this might be done without falling into the trap of presenting Mass as purely an entertainment is beyond the scope of this article, but it is a challenge that needs to be undertaken in a serious manner if we are to engage with the young, and perhaps not so young, generations in the modern world.

Notes

1   F. Burch Brown, *Religious Aesthetics: A Study of Making and Meaning* (Princeton: Princeton University Press, 1989), 78, 79.
2   Ibid., 86.
3   W. H. McCabe, *An Introduction to Jesuit Theatre* (St Louis: The Institute of Jesuit Sources, 1983), 25.
4   Ibid., 25.
5   Barrault, *The Uses of Drama*, 28.
6   R. Otto, *The Idea of the Holy*, trans. John W. Harvey (London: Oxford University Press) 3.
7   R. Viladesau, *Theology and the Arts: Encountering God through Music, Art and Rhetoric* (New Jersey: Paulist Press, 2000) 219.
8 · Otto, *The Idea of the Holy*, 65.
9   L. B. Gilkey, 'Can Art Fill the Vacuum?' in *Art, Creativity and the Sacred*, ed. D. Apostolos-Cappadona (New York: Crossroad, 1988) 189.
10   Ibid. 189
11   Pope John Paul II, *Letter to Artists* (http://www.vatican.va/holy_father /john_paul_ii/letters/documents/hf_jp-ii_let_23041999_artists_en.html).
12   See B. Flanagan, *The Spirit of the City: Voices from Dublin's Liberties* (Dublin: Veritas, 1999), 6 ff.
13   H. G. Gadamer, 'The Festive Character of Theatre' in *The Relevance of the Beautiful and Other Essays*, trans. Nicholas Walker, Ed. R. Bernasconi (Cambridge: Cambridge University Press, 1986), 65.
14   Ibid. 64.
15   G. G. May, *Will and Spirit: A Contemplative Psychology* (New York: HarperCollins, 1982) 108.
16   Ibid. 109.
17   K. Rahner, *Theological Investigation, Vol. XXIII*, trans. H. M. Riley & J. Donceel (London: Darton Longman and Todd, 1992) 164.
18   B. Brown, *Religious Aesthetics*, 88.
19   H. Urs Von Balthasar, *Theo-Drama Theological Dramatic Theory, Vol 1, Prolegomena*, trans. Graham Harrison (San Francisco: Ignatius Press, 1988) 112.
20   Gadamer, *Relevance of the Beautiful*, 65, 64.
21   G. E. Thiessen, *Theology and Modern Irish Art* (Dublin: Columba Press, 1999) 269.
22   Gilkey, in *Art and the Sacred*, 189.
23   See Otto, *The Idea of the Holy*, 64, 65.

Contemplating Dying When God is Distant

NUALA ROTHERY

In Ireland today there are a growing number of people who do not attend any religious service on a regular basis, and who would, in fact, classify themselves as not belonging to any religion. In view of the fact that I myself fall into this category, and that many of my friends do as well, it occurred to me to wonder how we would approach the idea of our inevitable deaths. I decided that this would be an interesting research project in applied spirituality.

In order to carry it out, I enlisted the help of a group of these friends, and asked for their assistance in a co-operative inquiry. They agreed with enthusiasm. Co-operative inquiry is a process where a group endeavours to research a question together. In considering the subject of death we explored a range of subjects from suicide and depression to our concept of God, and in particular, to what gives meaning to our lives.

Background

There have been very significant changes in society in the last thirty years. In Ireland families are smaller; more women work outside the home; attendance at religious services has dropped and the power of the established Church has diminished considerably. According to an IMS Survey, reported in *The Irish Times* in September 2002, the attendance figure at religious services at that time was down to 48 per cent of the population and 32 per cent of Irish people have their own set of beliefs that don't fully conform to any particular set of teachings. Many people die in hospital rather than at home, and the rituals around death are no longer practised as in the past. Bodies are removed from hospital to the mortuary rather than to the person's home and the traditional wake is now a rarity, particularly in urban areas.

I wanted to look at the subject of death, dying and preparation for death, and it occurred to me to wonder how these inevitable events impacted on the many non-practising people who come to that point in their lives where the idea of their own dying begins to come closer. I have no doubt that many will revert to the religious practices of their childhood and early life. But there must be a significant number for whom this avenue would not be possible, among whom I would number myself, and many of my friends.

Methodology

Classically, co-operative inquiry goes through four stages. Firstly a group gathers together with a view to partaking in the research. Initial discussion of an agreed topic is followed by the making of a plan for exploring the topic, and arrangements are made to schedule further meetings. In the second stage the participants carry out their agreed actions. Stage three involves the group becoming fully immersed in the experience. New ideas and creative insights may emerge. In the fourth stage, the group meets again to share their experience and consider what amendments they may need to make to their original ideas.

I chose to work with a group of friends who have met regularly as a reading group since 1991. We have covered a wide range of topics, many of them related to personal development, spirituality and psychotherapy. All of us are women. We come from very different backgrounds and have different levels of education. The group varies in age from forty-seven to sixty-nine. We have known each other for varying lengths of time. All have been actively engaged in their own development for at least twenty years. As a group we are accepting and supportive of one another, but we also have very different opinions on many subjects, which we are not afraid to express. We are accustomed to challenging one another and to working at a deep level in our discussions. There are also several members of the group who are highly skilled facilitators with creative talents, which could benefit the research. The subject of death and our own persona in dying is arresting, to say the least. It would be surprising if it did not bring up strong feelings in all of us. As a group we were well used to working with our feelings, and were not afraid of them.

Death

Echoing Freud, Becker says that 'Of all things that move man, one of the principal ones is his terror of death'.[1] As human beings we have a unique awareness of the fact of our own mortality, and both Freud and Becker hold that from an early age children are conscious of this fact, and are terrified by it. 'There really was no way to overcome the dilemma of existence, the one of the mortal animal who at the same time is conscious of his mortality.'[2] Yalom echoes the same theme when he says that 'a core existential conflict is the tension between the awareness of the inevitability of death and the wish to continue to be.'[3] He outlines some basic principles.

The fear of death plays a major role in our internal experience; it haunts as does nothing else; it rumbles continuously under the surface; it is a dark unsettling presence at the rim of consciousness.

The child, at an early age, is pervasively preoccupied with death, and his or her major developmental task is to deal with terrifying fears of obliteration. To cope with these fears, we erect defences against death awareness, defences that are based on denial, that shape character structure, and that, if maladaptive, result in clinical syndromes. In other words, psychopathology is the result of ineffective modes of death transcendence.[4]

This reality can be readily seen in the reluctance most people have when faced with any mention of death. In speaking about my research on the subject to friends or acquaintances, the reaction of many was one of rejection of any possible discussion about it. They seemed amazed that anyone would deliberately choose to think about it. However, Catholics are reminded of their impending deaths every time they say the *Hail Mary*, and every Ash Wednesday. 'Remember man thou art but dust and into dust thou shalt return,' and Buddhist monks and nuns meditate on it every day of their lives.

In an interesting article devoted to 'Spiritual Issues in Death and Dying for Those Who do not have Conventional Belief,'[5] Paul Irion points out that:

> Human beings, as part of the natural order are dying all the time they are living. Only as one becomes aware of this fact and accepts it, does personal existence assume a new quality. Death is still very real, a tragic threat which hangs over life, but life reaches its fullness through acceptance of the fact of this death.

This coincides with the view of many other writers that it is in facing the reality of our dying that we learn to live more fully. 'Lifelong consideration of death enriches rather than impoverishes life. Although the physicality of death destroys man, the idea of death saves him.'[6]

Elisabeth Kubler-Ross devoted her life to working with the dying. She has been enormously influential in shaping our ideas of how to enable people who are dying to do so with dignity and with as little pain as possible. She gave the following as her final word on the subject:

> Death can show us the way, for when we know and understand completely that our time on earth is limited, and that we have no way of knowing when it will be over, then we must live each day as if it were the only one we had.[7]

Structure of Investigation

For this essay I intend to identify the group only by coded initials, E, F, G, Q, Y and R (myself).

We held an initial meeting where we decided on the structure of the research. The group agreed that we would hold a workshop for a full day to consider the question. We would later have another shorter meeting to reflect on what had happened and give feedback. Y suggested that before the workshop day we complete an exercise called 'The Gospel of My Life'. This is in the nature of a reflection on many aspects of life which a person might consider on the last day of their lives. I give 'The Gospel' in full below. I was grateful for Y's suggestion, as I felt that reflecting on our lives as if we were leaving them would focus the group on the subject.

The Gospel of My Life
Imagine that this is the last day of your life:

1   These things I have loved in life; things I have tasted, seen, smelt, heard, touched:
2   These things have liberated me:
3   These beliefs I have outgrown:
4   These convictions I have lived by:
5   These things I have lived for:
6   These experiences I have cherished:
7   These insights I have arrived at in my life, about God, human nature, love:

8   These risks I have taken:
9   These sufferings have seasoned me:
10   These lessons life has taught me:
11   These influences (persons, events, occupations, books) have shaped my life:
12   These ideas have inspired me:
13   These things I regret about my life:
14   These are my life achievements:
15   These persons are enshrined in my heart:
16   These are my unfulfilled desires:
17   These are the things that have given my life meaning:
18   These are my thoughts and feelings about death.

At our preliminary meeting there was some significant discussion and deep sharing on the subject of death, dying and the prospect of doing the research. Various members of the group expressed what they would like to get from participating in the research.

On the workshop day we all faced an awareness of suicide and death. We were precipitated into it by Y, who did not attend the workshop, but sent a letter telling us that she was close to suicide. This evoked a powerful response in all of us. The resulting discussion explored the reality of living with deep depression, which most of the group had experienced. E spoke about 'the isolation of the black depths which she had lived through'. On the other hand, the thought of death as a way out could be enticing. G had seen 'the attraction of dying and perhaps going to a better place.' However, that depended entirely on what a person believes would happen after death. A contrary view was expressed by F. 'Suicide prevented by fear that the nightmare would continue, perhaps worse, perhaps unabated after death.' The conclusion reached by most, as Y had written was that 'It's harder to live than it is to die.'

Suicide and Depression

The rate of suicide in Ireland has been increasing alarmingly in recent years. According to statistics issued by the Central Statistics Office there were 354 suicides in 1992, compared with 448 in 2001. Of these, fifty-four were women in 1992, and ninety-two in 2001. So while the figure for males has increased by about a third, that for females has almost doubled. As, in my professional experience, more women suffer from depression than men, perhaps this is not surprising. As Q said 'That such a high proportion of us have felt the desire to die and put an end to our suffering probably indicates that this phenomenon is widespread, but secret, in our culture.' It is also well known that an attempt at suicide is a cry for help.

Denial of the reality of death is common in our culture. The focus for many is on material success, achievement in the world, the attainment of status in one way or another. F had identified herself as a 'depressed automaton walking around'. She had tried *to* 'let go of her addiction to work and success', without perhaps realising that this addiction may have been an attempt to distract herself from the realisation of death, which in itself may have led to depression. Hillman says that in attempting to deny the reality of their inevitable deaths, many fall into deep depression, which he sees as 'an attempt to understand death by joining it.'[8]

When we consider the description of depression by Gerald Priestland, perhaps the choice of suicide becomes more understandable. Depression is like a dark mist lurking in the corners of the room, always there, always ready to come surging forward and rising up to envelop you. It is blackness, it is emptiness, it is meaninglessness and total inner despair.[9]

My reading, however, has consistently pointed to the positive nature of depression as a catalyst for change in the individual. Thomas Moore argued that there might be a purpose in depression. In *Care of the Soul* he says:

> Faced with depression, we might ask ourselves, 'What is it doing here? Does it have some necessary role to play?' Especially in dealing with depression, a mood close to our feelings of mortality, we must guard against the denial of death that is so easy to slip into. Even further, we may have to develop a taste for the depressed mood, a positive respect for its place in the soul's cycles.[10]

He and many others (for example, Scott Peck, Kubler-Ross, Yalom) focus on the turning point that depression can be in terms of personal growth. A person suffering from depression is faced with the depths of their own being, and the only way out seems to be that of accepting the need for change, however difficult that may be. This leads inevitably to the growth in the person of individuality and non-conformity which may not be socially acceptable, and can be a dangerous option. This was recognised by E when she said 'Who do I know that I can feel safe to allow my wild self to be let out with?' Obviously, she did not feel safe to reveal this part of herself where it would not be accepted. It takes a great deal of courage to release oneself from established norms, and allow oneself to be different. It may result in a person being misunderstood or possibly ostracised by society. Standing alone can be very uncomfortable, which is why a support group, such as we have, is so important.

However, the real difficulty is in facing into the black depths of despair that living with depression involves. The pervasiveness of feelings of depression in the group was strong, and Hamlet's dilemma 'Whether to take arms against a sea of troubles, and by opposing end them' had been known to most of them. The relationship between depression and mortality and personal growth work was also clear. Scott Peck says:

> People feel depressed when they think they are in a trap, a cage from which they can see no way out. Frequently, however, at least some of the bars of the cage are of their own making. Usually such bars represent something to which they are excessively attached: a role, a person, often a dream or fantasy. Depression is useful because its pain is a signal to us that we need to give something up; the depression provides a motive for us to do the psychological work of relinquishing that person or that role. Consequently, I have written of the 'healthiness of depression'. It frequently inspires people to psychospiritual growth and the creation of positive changes in their lives.[11]

In facing their fear of death, and their real experience of depression, the workshop day provided an opportunity for the members of the group to acknowledge the fear, share feelings about depressive illness, and gain support from each other in that sharing. As a result of the workshop E recorded 'I felt very alive and real and safe and free to be able to articulate my own journey of near suicides, depressions and the shame of resorting to anti-depressants and alcohol at times to cope with the pain of *living*'.

On relating the finding that depression is an opportunity for growth to the group at a later meeting, I was surprised to find that they unanimously agreed with this idea, however painful their experience has been.

An awareness of death was present in the group, for some combined with a deeply felt fear. Y 'The thought of death terrifies me', but aligned to that was the fear that 'I might die before I've lived', which the research helped to highlight. This thought was very evident in the discussion that followed receiving her letter, which seemed to threaten suicide. It was the need to really live before we died that was uppermost in people's minds.

The realisation that we were not fully living was brought home to all of us during our discussions on the day, and resulted in a determination to change in such a way as to immerse ourselves in life to the fullest degree possible.

G admitted that 'Death. I am afraid. No – I am not ready to die.' She has had no direct experience of death, except in the sense that each loss can be seen as a little death, and this she was aware of. Q, on the other hand, has had several of those close to her die in the recent past. She saw that 'Death is in the field....For me it reinforces a sense of time running out – that the years remaining to me are precious, and that I want to courageously seek out something more fulfilling than my present way of life.'

The Use of Anti-Depressants

Acknowledging their experience of depression and looking deeply into it had alerted two members of the group to the problem of how they might manage it. Both E and G spoke of the shame they felt in taking anti-depressants, which was powerful, and also of the perception that anti-depressants suppressed feeling. However, they differed in their reaction to this. G decided to relinquish anti-depressants, in order to face 'the reality of trying to live fully.' E, on the other hand was very glad to have them. She spoke of the 'isolation of the black depths which I have lived through, but which are now held in check by taking anti-depressants.' She has found that for her they make living possible. For the rest of the group, who were not faced with this decision, the issue was much more about finding meaning in life, and how that might be done. Belief in God or lack of it was important here.

Concepts of Spirituality and God

In reviewing my record of the day, I find that the word spirituality is barely mentioned in the text, and then primarily by me. Nevertheless, I maintain that this is a deeply spiritual group. In his introduction to the subject of spirituality in the Summer School held at the Milltown Institute in 2001, Fr Jack Finnegan used this definition (among many):

Spirituality is understood as basic life orientation, as having to do with the essence of existence, the fundamental meaning making process of life.[12]

He emphasised the fact, over and over again, that living spiritually means being committed to awareness and reflection. It also involves relationship, ecology, creativity and care for both self and other. Above all, it is an expression of love in action.

I think it is self-evident that this group, in that sense, is deeply spiritual. However, the degree to which God, as a concept, is evident in their lives is problematic. Dermot Lane states that:

The question of God is the ultimate question of life; it is the single most important question facing men and women in the world today.[13]

This does, of course, depend on what we mean by the word God. Throughout history people have struggled to define what they mean by God. Their interpretations have changed many times over, as evidenced by Karen Armstrong's thoroughly researched book on the subject *A History of God*.[14] In later life, Armstrong discovered, to her surprise, that 'instead of waiting for God to descend from on high, I should deliberately create a sense of him for myself'. She goes on to say that her reading led her to believe that clerics of various religions:

would have taken me to task for assuming that God was – in any sense – a reality 'out there'; they would have warned me not to expect to experience him as an objective fact that could be discovered by the ordinary rational process. They would have told me that in an important sense God was a product of the creative imagination, like the poetry and music that I found so inspiring. A few highly respected monotheists would have told me quietly and firmly that God did not really exist – and yet that 'he' was the most important reality in the world.[15]

There's an in-built contradiction which demands exploration. Armstrong dismisses any idea of a concrete definition of God, and yet holds that God was 'the most important reality in the world'. I found this thinking very helpful. Somehow the paradox makes sense to me.

Armstrong claims 'human beings are spiritual animals ... Men and women started to worship gods as soon as they became recognisably human.'[16] Later she says that:

> The fact that people who have no conventional religious beliefs should keep returning to central themes that we have discovered in the history of God, indicates that the idea is not as alien as many of us assume. Yet during the second half of the twentieth century, there has been a move away from the idea of a personal God.[17]

Billington has written a book whose avowed aim is to declare God redundant. He claims:

> Religion is not a gift bestowed upon grateful receivers by an act of revelation from on high: it is a natural part of human experience which embraces many more people than actually claim to be religious.[18]

The last thing the research group would claim to be would be religious. Nevertheless, they certainly share in the search for meaning in their lives which both of these authors cite as a quintessential part of the human condition.

The image of God as a lawgiver, ready to punish us with hell fire and damnation; watching our every move, is not one which many in today's world would wish to adhere to. Even God the Father as a benevolent figure looking down from above has limited appeal. F echoed this when she said that 'God as an old man on a white cloud means absolutely nothing to me'.

In the research group a belief in a defined deity was almost completely absent. Nevertheless, we were all involved in what Dermot Lane calls 'the restless searchings of the human spirit.'[19] G: 'It's going to the well and letting down a bucket, but there's no water in the well. The water is below ground level, and you're dying of thirst in the desert. If you stand still you really have to look at the emptiness.' There are echoes here of nada, the dark night of the soul, and the spiritual dryness so consistently recorded by the mystics. F also realised that 'It's not enough to just stop doing'. She had found that having let go of work and success and having looked within, 'there's nothing there.' I had had very similar experience in my own life. These were further examples of the emptiness of which G had spoken.

For me there is a question here about the distinction between spiritual desolation and depression. In order to transcend the ego and reach the true self, we must overcome the ego's control needs, power needs and approval seeking needs. This is where the work lies. To live spiritually is to be committed to awareness. However, a person pursuing this path can still sleep, eat and laugh. It is this rootedness in reality which, he said, distinguishes spiritual transformation from depression, which is a psychiatric disorder.[20] Using this definition, it seems to me that my research group are doing the work of transformation rather than suffering from psychiatric illness. I cannot vouch for their sleep patterns, but they can certainly eat and laugh. However, whether we look on depression as spiritual transformation, or as an opportunity for growth, it seems that it can have more positive connotations than those usually attributed to it.

The value of doing the research was noted by Q. She said that awareness of death 'increases the value of life and being alive, or causes us to question the meaning of existence, whether there are forces such as Good and Evil, God or the Devil.' Julie Neuberger spells out how best to proceed:

> We will only die better, and grieve better, if we are prepared to talk about it now... in our homes, our schools, our churches, mosques, temples and synagogues. We will only achieve a real change, allowing ourselves to express our fears and hopes and desires, if we are prepared to face the issue of how best to meet our end...[21]

The opportunity to do this was much appreciated by the entire group. Perhaps I was the only person present who has a strong belief in God, but that belief is for me, as for the others, shrouded in mystery. I said that 'My concept of God was very nebulous. It was more like God is life or energy.' F found this idea more useful than the traditional model of God mentioned above. However, she still had a real difficulty, as she had 'no belief either in God or the devil.' She repeated the remark attributed to Rahner 'If you haven't experienced God no amount of someone else telling you will help to get you there.' She also spoke of looking within and finding 'nothing there'. However, her reflections on the day seemed to promise real change in letting go of old attitudes and compulsions and living more holistically. E focused on the question which has puzzled so many. 'What is God and how does that understanding impact on our day-to-day living?' Perhaps Armstrong's thoughts, quoted above, might be helpful for her. The necessity to be explicit and concrete in one's ideas about God is essentially a lost cause, since God is ultimate mystery and cannot be defined by the human intellect. If we can let go of the need for a concrete definition, perhaps it may be easier for this group to live with the possibility of the reality of God.

For most of the group, the search for meaning was by far the more important question. Whether this also was a search for God was not at all clear. It was, perhaps, for some, but irrelevant for others.

Meaning of Our Lives

According to Erikson, the last stage of psychosocial development is the negotiation of integrity versus despair. The realisation that four of the six members of this group were struggling with that dichotomy was startling. Q and I would seem to have resolved it, but the other members of the group were living it on a day to day basis. Perhaps I should not have been surprised, as the resolution of this stage is most likely to come as one gets older. Q and I are the oldest members of this group, and thus have had more time to come to terms with it.

Elizabeth MacKinlay defines several themes as the Spiritual Tasks of Ageing:

- to transcend disabilities and loss;
- to search for final meanings
- to find intimacy with God and/or others;
- to find hope.[22]

The search for meaning; finding intimacy; and finding hope were very evident in our discussions. E defined her needs. 'I want to love and be loved; I want to feel and think and be able to share these thoughts and feelings with others and vice versa; I want "Fun" and "Laughter" in my life.'

'The Gospel of My Life Exercise' had the effect of making people think about their lives, and how they were living them. This was very difficult for some members of the group, as it tended to throw up negative rather than positive aspects of their lives. It also focused attention on what was meaningful for them. This search for meaning was a central part of the discussion on the workshop day, and was closely allied with the concept of God, and whether or not a belief in

God (however understood) enabled people to live with greater ease and at peace with themselves.

However, from the very beginning it was evident that the search for meaning in our lives was of paramount importance. At our first planning session, E said 'If I can learn something that would help me to change my life and give more meaning to it, it would be worth it.' And again 'What are our criteria for meaningful living?' F agreed. 'What would be enough to leave behind? What was the significance in my living?'

In focusing attention on the reality of our own inevitable deaths, the members of the group were forced to confront their fears, (G 'Fear – I am afraid') and to struggle towards finding meaning in lives which were lived in what is known as the 'real world'. Facing these fears and expressing them enabled a degree of sharing which was intensely liberating. As E said, Y's letter 'threw us immediately and deeply into a discussion on life; on the meaning of life, how to live in this world of today, how to make sense of it all.'

Stephen Levine says that:

> Resistance to the pain about us causes the heart to wither. Allowing that pain to enter into us tears our heart open and leaves us exposed to the truth.[23]

In this workshop, I think it is evident that pain entered into all of us, and that we were exposed to the truth within ourselves. In fact, focusing on death brought us into reflection on life. The feedback after the workshop day confirmed the very real benefit that had been gained by members of the group.

For all of us, the search for our individual spiritual paths (however defined) has been, and remains, a crucially important part of our lives. This is closely linked with our search for authenticity, and our endeavours to extract ourselves from the tyranny of 'niceness' with which we had all been brought up. E 'saw the danger that in playing the "nice" role we lose our authenticity.' This was a very strong theme in the follow-up meeting, and was shared by all of us. Allowing ourselves to feel negative emotions and express our anger or hurt has not been felt to be socially acceptable. In the endeavour to retain the good opinion of others we have, from time to time, sacrificed our real selves. This was recognised and owned by all. The recognition in itself is a catalyst for change.

Conclusions

In working with this group there was an unusual degree of openness and honesty which resulted in a profound sharing of personal material, and, I think, a consequent degree of healing.

One of the strong themes that emerged in the last meeting of the group was the need to forego 'being nice'. We have all grown up in a society where women have been conditioned to be attentive to the needs of others and to refrain from expressing their own needs, or expect to have them met. Nevertheless, I think there is no doubt that in our search for meaning and authenticity, we as a group are remarkably open, and provide a high degree of loving support for one another, which will only be enhanced by greater honesty.

Effect on the Participants

It seems that participation in the workshop has enabled a certain amount of transformation in the research group. It has helped us to clarify various aspects of our lives. In particular, the way we live whatever time remains to us became a primary concern for each of us. It is difficult to say how much the workshop had to do with the very substantial changes each of us has made. The experience of taking a long, hard look at the reality of the limited time we have left to us, gave an impetus to our decision making and helped individuals to clarify what it is they really want from what is left of their lives.

For myself, I realised only towards the end of this process that my decision to research this subject, and to involve my friends in it, was an attempt to come to terms with my own ageing and dying, and that I needed support in so doing. The experience has been an extremely positive one. In my widespread reading on the subject, I found constant reiteration of the fact that looking at dying enables the individual to live more fully. To use the time I have left in the best possible way has become my aim. If I can live every day as if it were my last I will pay attention to my inner self, follow my heart and do only what seems right. For me it's a very satisfactory conclusion to a period of intensive study.

Notes

1   E. Becker, *Denial of Death* (New York: Free Press Paperbacks, 1973), 11.

2   Ibid., 268.

3   I.D. Yalom, *Existential Psychotherapy* (New York: Basic Books, 1980), 8.

4   Ibid., 27.

5   K.J. Doka, J.D. & Morgan (eds.), *Death and Spirituality* (Death Value and Meaning Series), (New York: Baywood Pub. Co. Inc., 1992), 93-112 at 104.

6   I.D. Yalom, *Existential Psychotherapy* (New York: Basic Books 1980), 30.

7   E. Kubler-Ross, (ed.), *Death – The Final Stage of Growth*, (New York: Touchstone – Simon & Schuster, Inc., 1975), 160.

8   J. Hillman, *Suicide and the Soul* (Connecticut: Spring Publications Incorporated, 1997), 63.

9   G. Priestland in *The Listener* (October 1980), p 538 cited by D. Rowe, *Depression,* 1983, (repr. 2002), 6.

10   T. Moore, *Care of the Soul – How to Add Depth and Meaning to Your Everyday Life* (London: Piatkus, 1992), (repr. 1994), 137.

11   M. Scott Peck *Denial of the Soul, Spiritual and Medical Perspectives on Euthanasia and Mortality* (New York: Harmony Books 1997) 73.

12   J. Finnegan, 'Some Themes in Contemporary Irish and European Spirituality', Milltown Summer School, 2001, 1.

13   D. Lane, *The Experience of God – An Invitation to do Theology* (Dublin: Veritas, 1985) 1.

14   K. Armstrong, *A History of God* (London: Vintage, 1999).

15   Ibid., 3-4.

16   Ibid., 3.

17   Ibid., 446.

18   R. Billington, *Religion without God* (London: Routledge, 2002).

19   D. Lane, *The Experience of God – An Invitation to do Theology* (Dublin: Veritas, 1985) 2.

20   J. Finnegan, 'Some Themes in Contemporary Irish and European Spirituality' (Summer School, Milltown Institute, 2001).

21   J. Neuberger, *Dying Well – A Guide to Enable a Good Death,* (Cheshire: Hochland & Hochland Ltd., 1999) 97.

22   Ibid., 224-226.

23   S. Levine, *Who Dies? – An Investigation of Conscious Living and Conscious Dying* (Anchor Books, New York: Doubleday, 1982) 170.

Sexuality, Gender and Spirituality

Eileen Pugh

The stone that the builders have rejected for so long, is in fact, a corner stone.

Ps 118:22, paraphrased by Eileen Pugh

Christianity is founded on the 'Word Made Flesh' and Jesus came that we may have life, and have it abundantly (Jn 10:10), yet it can be difficult to discover how the flesh of sexuality and words of spirituality are interrelated so as to give life. These two dimensions of the self are impoverished however in absence of each with the other. In attending to this issue I am unable to be objective or neutral. It is out of the acceptance of the beauty of the Word Made Flesh that I was drawn to write this essay. The truth can set us free, I believe, if we have the courage to face up to our uneasiness and to allow a sense of our bodies re-emerge as temples of the Holy Spirit.

My personal history as a wife and mother will not be excluded although I attempt, through awareness of my assumptions and personal involvement, to use my own reactions critically in seeking insight. It was my personal spiritual/sexual experience that impelled me to question the present diminished position sexuality often inhabits who Christianity. Meeting others on the spiritual path that yearned for affirmation of their sexuality as intrinsic to their spirituality confirmed for me the vacuum that exists. I have also encountered desolation in those who cannot identify positively with a single gendered God or an asexual holy family.

Understanding how perspectives that denigrated sexuality arose historically can make way for forgiveness and reconciliation. It is imperative to look back on our history in order to understand how and why we have arrived at the present dilemma. In so far as possible I take a non-judgmental stance, seeking to understand and not to blame. My motivation is the discovery of authentic sources for a spirituality of sexuality. The hope is also to provoke collaborative, genuine, honest, open discussion.

I am not, however, intent on promoting sexuality as having solely positive aspects. It would be best to ignore the surplus of undermining distortions in pornography, trafficking and the sex trade. In a small way, I aim to explore possibilities of releasing the marginalised sacred dimension of the sexual aspect of our human experience.

In discussing sexuality I will not be referring to genitalisation alone, but sexuality as involving the whole person – the physical, emotional and psychological experience of being a sexual human being. An unhealthy preoccupation with purity or with all things sexual can both result in a rejection of the inner core of our being as contaminated. It is incredible to observe the gap that persists between the sexual and the holy, and the desolation and fragmentation in the human person that this gap can create. The urgency and appeal I have encountered in those who have shared their experience motivated me to undertake this essay. What possibility is there to look at unhealthy sexuality if we do not collaborate to penetrate decades of silence surrounding what largely remains an unspoken healthy sexuality? The aim of this essay is to encourage and assist those on a spiritual path to make an honest effort to reclaim and integrate sexuality into their spiritual lives.

Sexuality

The word sexuality comes from the Latin '*secare*' meaning 'to cut' or 'to divide.' Sexuality suggests then an experience of incompleteness seeking wholeness and connection that reaches beyond our differences and divisions. Sexuality is a strange and mysterious aspect of our human nature. In Greek mythology, Eros was the god of sexual passion, the son of Aphrodite the goddess of desire. The energy of *eros* is characterised by passion, ecstasy, madness and irrationality. *Eros* brings pain and suffering. The problems of eros persist today. On the other hand, *eros* can be seen as a fundamental spiritual impulse to reach out beyond ourselves for connection, to become vulnerable, often against our defensive instincts. Trusting and surrendering to body talk holds a possibility for deeper communication.

It would be naïve however to ignore the dilemmas created by *eros*. We can be overwhelmed by its power of seduction and enticement. It challenges us to embrace the mysterious paradox of both anxiety and pleasure. Erotic living involves an expanded awareness. It will open the way to being self-revealed. The consequence of unawareness is lack of self-knowledge. The frustration of this experience of alienation may equally result in inner torment and destruction, both for ourselves and others.

Opening ourselves to the thoughts, feelings, longings that are embedded in sexual fear and regret provides a path to healing. Sexuality in its fullest sense is creative spirit. Sexuality is the energy drive toward creation, procreation, growth and fullness of life. A thawing-out and integration of sexuality is a fundamental concomitant of spiritual growth.[1]

Spirituality

Spirituality, as used here, embraces all aspects of our lives. Spiritual development takes place in a context immersed in culture, society and personal history. Contemporary culture is commodity driven; spirituality and sexuality are among the consumerist commodities available. From this perspective it may be said that we have become over-sexed and obsessed with shape and size in a way that exploits both men and women. There is so much inherited embarrassment, so much unsaid, ignorance rather than innocence and double standards for males and females.

The media has addressed many pertinent issues such as gender oppression, sexual orientation, sexually transmitted diseases, sexual abuse, and fertility management. There is, from some quarters, much criticism of media for promoting promiscuity and permissiveness, for degrading men and women through advertising, for sexualising children, and for the ongoing devaluing of the human person. This media activity may be an inevitable reaction against past repression. We must ask if we have moved from a sense of human beings as bodiless spirits to spiritless bodies.

In contrast the path of spirituality focuses on the whole experience of the human person as the place of meeting with God. Spirit pervades every dimension of our lives whether we acknowledge it or not. There is a profound need for spirituality to embrace sexuality. Emphasising that we are in fact embodied spirits helps to illuminate the vital importance of creating a sacred space to listen to our sexuality.

Being alive is being sexual whether we are celibate or in a committed relationship. It is not possible to be spiritual and not sexual, both penetrate all existence. All making of connections involves sexual energy, the energy of connection whether this relating is towards God, nature or other persons. We can frequently be unaware of the dynamic force attracting and drawing us. Can we dare to take a closer look? Fear, repression and ignorance need to be met with compassion if transformation is to take place. Awakening what lies beneath, befriending the lost *eros* energy, awaiting as mystery unfolds, needs unconditional loving respect. Experiences of discomfort, inhibition, turmoil guilt and shame can become part of a radical process of conversion and integration.

Here I am not exclusively concerned with consummated relationships, but the many forms of mutual relationships. Intimacy in soul sharing by which we reveal our naked, vulnerable selves to others involves our sexuality. We reach out aching for connection, yearning for the inner completeness that arises from being heard and understood. Excessive fear of the perils of sexual passion can result in shallowness or hypocrisy in relationships or a diminished experience of the love of God coming to us in the experience of friendship.

The process of inner questioning will necessarily lead to struggling with shadows. A willingness to take a fresh look at inherited attitudes that can lie behind the inner turmoil will be necessary if inner harmony is to be achieved. The journey towards wholeness involves the process of embracing those aspects of ourselves that we have disowned or orphaned, but which continue to live on in spite of us.

Reflecting on our image of God will be vital for this spiritual transformation. Our deepest desire is to know and be known. This is a challenge, as rejection is always a possibility. I have been amused when reflecting that God's sense of humour involves situating our genitals directly beside the lowly elimination canal. How many of us have embedded labels such as 'dirty' or 'disgusting'? It is an interesting positioning. Can we embrace our bodies, accepting their sexual sensations and seek God through it all? Is it acceptable to reject such a gift from God? Can we give loving attention to sexual sensations when they permeate our physical body and ask where is God in this encounter? Or have we decided this is not and cannot be God's department? If so, is God a faulty creator, or are we at fault? Is our spirituality sanitised or all-inclusive?

The contemporary practice of spiritual direction must be open to exploring sexuality as an inherent expression of seeking God in all things. The paradox is that through personal taking hold of dysfunctional beliefs they can be deconstructed and released, enabling authentic mystery to be deepened and enhanced in the process. However, if spiritual directors do not integrate their own sexuality they will be unable to help those they accompany. Negative images of a male, omnipotent, judgmental God, primarily preoccupied with sexual sin, require substantial helpful intervention and spiritual healing. Spiritual directors may be of assistance to directees in naming God in their experience of desire, in thanking God for the gift of sexuality with its potential for deep loving relating. Such topics continue to remain a challenge and a threat for many spiritual directors. Given the trauma people can suffer in simply being unable to utter the labels for their genitals it is clearly evident that such people can be diminished and incapable of experiencing the abundant life Jesus desired for all.

The Journey of Integration: Questions for Reflection

Questioning our assumptions is vital to bring to awareness how we have been conditioned. Automatic responses have been formed. The questions below may be of assistance in noticing changes in understanding that have already happened as we developed from child to adult. They will lead us to reflect on who, what and where influenced these changes and whether they were helpful or unhelpful developments for us.

- In your early childhood, how was a spiritual sense experienced at home?
- What did you think about God? What was important?
- What were the attitudes around the body at home when you were a young child?
- How did school influence your understanding?
- How did you learn the facts of life?
- What does spirituality mean to you today?
- Do you relate scripture, prayer or God to your body; to your sexuality?
- What does sexuality mean to you today?
- How has your religious tradition influenced your sense of sexuality?
- How do the media portrayals of sexuality affect you?
- What concerns, if any, do you have around the connection between sexuality and spirituality?

We each have a unique personal life story. As we tell and retell these stories we gain further insight and come to realise we are not alone, rather we are all in an evolving journey together. There will be a need for compassion and reconciliation as we look at society and what it has failed to do. Attempting to discover truth takes courage. Sexual abuse is not within the scope of this essay and yet we have all suffered as victims of the ignorance generated by historical conditioning. It is a huge task to learn a new vocabulary and language in order to give voice to the search for God in uncharted lands.

Irish culture has undergone dramatic change over these past three decades. We have become increasingly aware of how taboo, stigma and gender discrimination have played harmful roles in the lives of men, women and children. Sexuality and spirituality have been in opposition. The bodyliness of the human condition has often been extremely problematic for anyone wanting to live a Christian life. There are now many varied understandings and representations of both spirituality and sexuality. As we try to exist in a chaotic divergence of contradictory ideas, a sense of a lost diamond in the psyche can arise. However, liberation from past repression and conditioning carries with it many growing pains. Movement towards autonomy can be a struggle. Competence in dialogue can only be gained through practice. An integrated spirituality in the future must envision the soul and the body as essential dual aspects of humanness and holiness. A spirituality that neglects this truth will inevitably be flawed. Perpetuating false truth by presuming sexually active people to be self indulgent, impure or defiled is no longer an option.

To heal the shame we have to look at our bodies lovingly. It is natural when attending to our bodies that sexual feelings may arise, but they will not compel us to respond to them; we just need to allow them to gift us and flow through. Paradigms are shifting. Belief systems can inhibit. Sexual wellness is unity of mind, body, and spirit.

The Christian Tradition on Sexuality
In the Song of Songs there is rich resource for beginning the journey.

> She says: 'For your lovemaking is better than wine.
> In fragrance, your oils are exquisite.' (Song 1: 2-3)
> He says: 'Your two breasts are like frisky fawns
> Lively gazelle twins.' (Song 4: 5)
> Many waters cannot quench love,
> Neither can floods drown it. (Song 8:7)

It can be challenging to encounter such explicit texts within the Bible, the word of God.

Less positively, in the Christian heritage sin has had a markedly sexual focus. Some representations of Mary as asexual and virginal together with some of the reflection in the past on the virginal conception of Jesus undermine the sexual identity of both men and of women. The impact on the Irish experience of sexuality of some preaching around these themes has been huge and many have had heavy burdens placed on their backs for a lifetime.

Dualism has also played havoc in Christianity. The Christian tradition has promoted celibacy as better than marriage, virgins as better than wives, men as better than women and spirit as better than body. Even sexual thoughts were a problem. Yet today we recognise the human person as a unity of body, mind, heart and spirit. Is it not time to take a refreshing look at the beginning experience of sexuality, awakening and arousal and the truth therein of a God constantly calling humanity to be attentive? It is remarkable how radiance oozes from those who have succeeded in embracing sexuality in a positive way.

In the majority of Christian societies for most of the last two thousand years males have dominated females. Male elevation to the exclusion of women has resulted in a degradation of both. It is critical that hearts be opened to the mystery indwelling in masculinity and femininity. Popular understanding of comments from Augustine and Aquinas such as the female being a 'defective male' have been a source of great pain.

The Body in Contemporary Spirituality

Against the background of the troubled history of the body the global embodied spirituality movement is giving rise to hopeful developments. The popularity of body arts such as massage, yoga and tai chi reflects an awareness of these arts as ways to practise both attention and listening through the body. As blocks and restrictions are noticed within the body focused awareness can direct to areas needing attention. The inner protest and persistent refusal of the body to be ignored is an innate part of being human.

Inevitably we will face the awakening of sexual energy while meditating. Sexuality is a fundamental life force. So we must ask if can see sexuality as our spiritual partner? Do we need to take responsibility for choosing in the past to shut God out of such deep experience? Trust, patience and wisdom are necessary to attempt to surrender and allow sensations and associated feelings to arise. As we become familiar with the inner touch of *eros* we learn to embrace the reality that sexual communication occurs on many levels.

Loving another person becomes a sacramental encounter of oneness with the sacred. Childhood trauma can play havoc with adult relationships. It is crucial for spiritual freedom and fulfilment that past debilitating attitudes be sensitively explored. Remembering must replace dismembering. The world will not end if you engage in sexual experience. I can think of sound reasons for choosing not to do so, but fear and disgust should not be among them. Our bodies are not pest houses. Genitals are simply part of a body: given to each of us, part of God's creation; a small part, true, but as real and as lovely as the rest. If you love every part, evil will not enter the world through us.

Conclusion

I have argued that an issue in need of urgent spiritual attention is the common social phenomenon of discomfort experienced when sexual matters are raised, particularly in a spiritual context. Genuine spirituality is and must be inclusive of the wide range of authentic human experience. No community or society can expect unwavering integrity. Contemplation is necessary to bring to awareness areas of vulnerability and brokenness in order to permit healing and repentance.

It is vital that the ongoing silence be broken in order to affirm ordinary people in their struggle. Those who have kept silent due to fear of recrimination and rejection must voice their personal experience and knowledge. True lovemaking is the work of the spirit, a precious life-giving experience to be embraced and applauded. In it we can see sexuality and spirituality as interdependent and complementary to each other.

A spirituality that denies sexuality is shallow and superficial. Sexually-denying spirituality echoes the urgency of the lost sheep or the missing coin gospel stories, a paradise lost. New strategies are necessary to reframe how we perceive and experience the relationship between sexuality and spirituality. A radical mind-shift can awaken us from the unconscious programming we have internalised. It is vital to bring out the unconsciously diseased and wounded aspect of both spirituality and sexuality and lay them before the passing presence of the Holy for healing. Perpetuation of negativity at best, or vacuum at worst, prevents a fullness of life experience.

This is an area of spirituality that largely remains unattended. It is both encouraging and yet alarming to realise how we influence and shape the internal experiences of others. It is crucial for spiritual flourishing to heal warped and impoverished understandings of the word made flesh in life. Workshops on sexuality, particularly for spiritual directors and those in pastoral ministry, could contribute to healing and integration.

Despite the so-called sexual liberation of contemporary society there is a long way to go to move from a superficial freedom to a liberation of depth. Intimacy with one's own sexuality must surely be a necessary ingredient in self-knowledge and fundamental to relating in a truly human way. If we, at worst, reject our body reactions or even remain neutral to tuning in we are denying the all-embracing scope of grace. To nurture awareness of body reactions to stimuli in everyday life is to enable a passionately discerning spirituality to be born. We need to shed unhelpful conditioning and lovingly attend to the creator's creation.

While I have discovered that the retrieval of positive traditions is well researched by academics it rarely, if ever, trickles through to ordinary, everyday situations. We are victims of victims. Perpetuating this ancient dichotomy should no longer be an option. In my experience, the negative indoctrination of shame and guilt associated with sexuality lies close to the surface. The immense harm perpetrated by Christian educators, including parents, can be accompanied by a deep anger. Strong feelings of anxiety, and at times even rage, at humiliation experienced in childhood has surfaced in many who have shared their stories. It is clear that many have also suffered degrees of emotional sexual abuse. This crisis is also an opportunity for immense healing. Spiritual and sexual illiteracy will continue if we do not face this, possibly daunting, but ultimately life-giving, undertaking. We need to foster an atmosphere of encouragement and discernment, to envisage a greater capacity for true relating and deeper intimacy with ourselves others and ultimately with the Divine.

This crisis is also a time of immense opportunity to reintegrate such a powerful human resource with vast healing power. The stone, which has been rejected for so long is, in fact, a corner stone.

Notes
1   G. May, *Will and Spirit* (San Francisco: Harper, 1982) 190.

Blessed Abundance: Ecological Spirituality in Ireland

Seán McKiernan

The Spirituality of Creation

People of faith believe that the spiritual dimension is the underlying factor present in creation. Matthew Fox suggests that creation is all things and us, that it is us in relationship with all things.[1] According to the author Thomas Berry behind all creation lies a core dimension, a psychic-spiritual reality.[2] He points to a numinous presence pervading the universe that is metaphorically expressed in various creation myths associated with the great world religions. Even physicists are now describing the universe in abstract rather than material terms. Indeed the most accurately scientific description of the physical universe currently available (quantum concept) demands that it be considered one whole, indivisible and conscious entity.[3] Although it is our present home, nevertheless Berry insists that the earth is an awesome mystery, but ultimately as fragile as ourselves. Understood from these perspectives, and bearing in mind that authentic spirituality is grounded in reality, I believe that caring for the earth's ecosystems is a spiritual as well as a physical way of upholding one's ultimate values.

Creation, the Earth and its Ecosystems

Having being raised on a farm, I developed a love for nature and the earth at an early age. Likewise as a Christian I acknowledge the marvels of creation – my basic introduction to the Divine, as revelations of God's power, wisdom and love. On planet Earth, it is evident that there is a definite interrelationship between all living things and their environment. This relationship and its scientific study is referred to as ecology. When applied to human societies, the author R.A. Simkins defines ecology as the way a society affects or is affected by its physical and biological environment.[4] The term 'ecology' is derived from the Greek 'oikos', meaning 'household' and it shares the same root word as 'economics.' Thus the term implies the study of the economy of nature. A group of clearly distinguished organisms, which interact with their environment as a unit, are generally referred to as an ecosystem. Within an ecosystem, everything depends upon everything else for survival and each ecosystem depends on all the others. All these systems combine to form the largest ecosystem, the earth itself – that planet capable of producing abundant food to meet the energy requirements of all its living entities. For these reasons one can appreciate the importance of the earth's ecosystems for maintaining life in its varied forms.

Destruction of the Ecosystems

Recently a large body of scientific evidence has found that humanity is causing widespread destruction to the earth's ecosystems. Scientists are predicting that this may have appalling consequences for all life on the planet. The World Watch Institute reports that the circumstances surrounding survival prospects for our species together with every other species has become less favourable over the last three decades. For a number of years now the anthropologist and author, Sean McDonagh, has been expressing concern about the rate of destruction of the earth by the human population.[5] Although the various industrial revolutions have delivered enormous benefits to about one-fifth of humanity he argues that the other four-fifths are being deprived of their rightful needs.

There is an inherent link between ecological issues and the concern for justice. All the evidence suggests that human society is recklessly polluting the earth's land-mass, the air and the water at an unprecedented rate. In so doing many of the earth's ecosystems are being altered or destroyed forever.

A New Vision

Just as earlier patterns of historical interpretation have arisen at times of stress to guide human affairs, so now a new vision is emerging to guide us – manifested in a world-wide movement, which is an ethical and moral response to this rapacious attitude to our earthly home. This comprises of various organisations that show concern for the welfare of the planet by a public response to the present crisis. The coming together of these organisations is broadly referred to as 'the ecological movement'.

By their caring attitude towards the earth, the people in this movement, often in difficult circumstances, appear to exhibit a spirit rarely experienced in contemporary society.

Inspired by these developments, I decided to research the spirituality of a group of people living within the ethos of the ecological movement. The case study involved conducting an in-depth interview with seven people based on prepared questions.

Hereunder are the names and age groups of the seven people that I interviewed. The names used are fictitious.

Name	Age Group
Ruth	40-49
Patrick	50-59
Angela	30-39
Matt	30-39
Dorothy	20-29
Keith	40-49
Christina	50-59

Self-Transcendence

To do this I began with Sandra Schneider's definition of spirituality as 'The experience of consciously striving to integrate one's life in terms not of isolation and self-absorption but of self-transcendence towards the ultimate value that one perceives.'[6]

My conversations suggested that the connection to the earth gave Ruth a sense of the internal connection to every other person at a deeper level. She contended that the further we go into ourselves, the more unified we become with humanity. Clearly Ruth is consciously striving to integrate her life in terms not of isolation and self-absorption, but towards self-transcendence by her desire for unity with all humanity.

From consciously striving to integrate her life with what she terms the 'ultimate presence', which she eventually found in nature and the earth, Ruth's image of God is stretched beyond human metaphors to contemplating the miracle of a tiny seed developing into a mature plant. An ultimate value for Ruth was for justice for all life forms – something she is consciously striving for. This endless quest leaves no room for becoming isolated or self-absorbed, instead it is a continual thrust that propels her outwards.

Shared System of Thought and Action

I then looked at the German psychoanalyst and author Eric Fromm's definition of spirituality as: 'A shared system of thought and action that gives adherence; a frame of orientation and devotion.'[7] He maintains that this system of thought is both philosophical (reason) and theological (love) and the actions are undertaken to improve the world, that is, moral actions.

From my findings it was obvious that Angela had a coherent system of thought and actions put in place. Angela expressed this by saying that the earth is central to our deliberations. By putting humankind at the centre, Angela proposes that this has created appalling consequences for everything on earth. She contended that the ecological movement is attempting to reverse this order, by placing the earth at the centre with humankind maintaining an important role in this reality. In her opinion this movement is endeavouring to alter the consciousness of society, so that it can work for all rights including human, animal, plant and water. In addition to human concerns these moral actions include concern for the welfare of every other species on earth. Her moral actions involve organic growing of chemical-free food in local areas, adopting natural waste-disposal methods, recycling waste material and community building.

Christian Spirituality

In 1987 Joan Wolski Conn wrote an article in the *New Dictionary of Theology* where she distinguishes spirituality as lived experience and from the academic discipline.[8] For most Christians spirituality means one's entire life, as understood, imagined, felt and decided upon in relation to the persons of the Trinity – Father, Son and Spirit.

Although words that contain Trinitarian dimensions occurred frequently throughout the interviews, Patrick was the only person to refer directly to this. 'Just by contemplating the life cycle of a plant, people can become inspired and learn a great deal about spirituality', he enthused. 'Becoming aware of a seed's potential and the manner in which it completes its life cycle should assist us in contemplating the Christian mysteries of life, death and rebirth.'

Nevertheless, bearing in mind the Christian upbringing of the interviewees, my research indicated that the institutional Church is failing to satisfy the spiritual hunger or deepest desires of the majority of these people. This failure to advocate and elucidate the connections between the human life cycle, the cycles of nature, and the life, death and resurrection of Jesus has been in my opinion a lost opportunity for Church.

Creation Spirituality

The next understanding that I found was 'creation spirituality', focused on and emphasising God as the creator of all things. This obligated humankind to care for all creation and to celebrate its goodness with expressions of joy, living our life in a humanised, communal and hospitable manner.

Indeed all the respondents frequently highlighted their awareness of the Creator and the sacredness of the call to care for the earth and all its inhabitants. Christina and Keith spoke of awe and wonder at the beauty of creation and the incredible power that holds it in existence. They both affirmed God as the creator, a spiritual presence underpinning all that exists. This motivates them in their work with the earth. Christina is convinced that God has made all things connect and viewed nature and the creator as beyond human understanding. Accepting and respecting this mystery, in Keith's opinion, is spiritual wisdom.

Failure to celebrate the earth's goodness with expressions of joy has saddened Dorothy: 'Not to celebrate the harvest in an agricultural country is astonishing', she remarks. Christina and Keith long for a community of like-minded people who will work for the earth and will celebrate its goodness.

From Desire to Action

In his book *The Holy Longing*, Ronald Rolheiser writes at length about spirituality as 'overcharged restlessness or desire' in each of us, an unquenchable flame, a longing, a disquiet or a hunger sometimes manifested in aching pain, other times as delicious hope. What we do, how we channel that *eros*, Rolheiser points out, is our spirituality. He contends that it is about being within community or else being lonely, about being in harmony with mother earth or else being alienated from her. Rolheiser believes that our desires basically shape our actions, our desires compel us to act, these action-shaping desires are our spirituality.

Ruth affirmed spirituality as the essence of a person, found in the heart and possessed by every living being. It is not intellectual, instead it concerns the qualities within the heart, ultimately relating to love. 'So again you could say that the desire for the good is an interconnectedness within humanity, a global sense', she says. 'Love is what unites us really', she concludes.

Ruth's desire for justice has acquired a new dimension since becoming more involved with the ecological movement, this unquenchable inner flame is burning more intensely than ever. Her actions contribute to community building, in harmony with the earth. Since becoming more involved Ruth has acquired a whole new passion and love for life and nature itself enabling her to live life with a greater sense of connectedness to everything.

This desire has caused her to abandon to a large extent post-modern culture, by opting out of mainstream society to embark on an alternative way of living.

Concerning Conversion

The theologian Donal Dorr,[9] writes about a balanced Christian spirituality modelled on a passage from the Book of Micah (Mc 6:8). In this text God makes three requests: (1) act justly, (2) love tenderly, (3) walk humbly with God. Dorr refers to spirituality as not just a set of theological ideas but more outlooks and attitudes that are revealed by the way we act and react. He suggests that this is an implicit theology that may become explicit by reflection and articulation, thus becoming authentic because it represents a truth that we live.

I noticed that Matt's creation spirituality emphasised space for reading, prayer and reflection. He articulated his ideas to groups and networks that he established.

Dorr quoting Micah referred to one's personal relationship with God, or personal religious conversion as 'walking humbly with God'. This sense of God's love and care changes the notion of providence into a living reality for interviewees.

The reference to humility connected with both Keith's and Ruth's assertion that organic living increases the virtue of humility in one's life. Matt realises that God keeps everything in existence, that everyone and everything is connected to God, carved in the palm of His hand. He emphasised utter dependence on God by referring to humankind as applying 'God's soil and water' to initiate propagation. Awareness of God's all-embracing plan motivates Matt to share his conversion experience with society and to strive to maintain work methods and systems that give a sense of connection to, and dependence on the creator. He pointed out that mechanisation and artificial fertilisation of the soil breaks the connection between people, the earth and its natural composting systems thereby cutting humanity off from its source and creator.

As an underpinning for this sense of Divine Providence, Dorr refers to a need for a certain peace and tranquillity that can be nourished by prayer. Matt's prayer time, as already noted, gives him this peace. 'The more you go into spirituality the more you give yourself time to be at peace with your God' he concluded.

From reflecting on her experience of working with the earth in prayer, Angela's sense of Divine Providence has developed and changed. 'The more we develop a spirituality of creation the more it changes and the deeper it becomes'.

God's call to love tenderly, as expressed by Micah, refers to the interpersonal aspect of Christian spirituality, the face-to-face relationships with other people.

In trying to establish a better world for everybody, even for future generations, Matt is surely answering the call to love tenderly. His plan for the future in sharing resources and establishing groups, illustrates his concern for the welfare of all peoples. 'We are tenants – we have been left the keys of the earth for the moment, and we must include the next generation in our plans', Matt concludes. Indeed Matt's increased love for the earth has enabled him to have an increased respect for every person. 'I suppose our relationship with the earth is reflected in everything that we do', he exclaims.

To act justly in Dorr's opinion, is a moral matter relating to the area of public life, the political sphere. His understanding of justice is primarily a concern with how society is organised, how wealth, power, rights and privileges are distributed to every level – local, national and global. As well as paying our debts and not stealing from others, justice also means working to build a society that contains just structures. Dorr refers to this as political conversion.

Matt perceives his work with the earth as a means to uphold justice. He believes that organic living helps to counteract the mindless manipulation of the earth by greedy people concerned only with profit, power and money. As a Christian he must see beyond these materialistic marketing ploys to work for justice for everyone, for the earth, indeed for all creation. He is adamant that Christianity, just action on behalf of nature, without diluting its core beliefs, should incorporate nature and the earth into its preaching.

Impact on Spirituality

In trying to ascertain the interaction between the ecological movement and different forms of spirituality I have discovered that the whole thrust central to the spirituality of those interviewed is a belief in the existence of a creator, a mysterious higher power totally beyond human understanding. I have learned that those who work in this movement continuously grapple with the scientific wonders of creation, indeed wonders that go beyond science – extending into mystery. They all have referred to this mystery in creation, even to the mystery of life itself.

Because they are deeply embedded in the ecological movement those people have acquired an overwhelming desire to respect the Creator; a respect that is amply borne out in their chosen lifestyles and thus reflected in an all-pervasive spirituality. Indeed, in the words of H.P. Santmire this spirituality is a reminder of the Celtic Saints' encounter with the enfleshed One (the Christ) from above, amidst the world of nature.[10] Not unlike the Celtic Saints, they too embrace nature with a profound sense of touching the Creator in their everyday lives. This movement has a major impact on the spirituality of its members today. Being involved with this movement increases their awareness of the mystery of creation, the life-cycle and the interconnectedness of all things. Consequently these people are more conscious of the impact of their own individual lifestyles, for better or worse, on creation, the earth in particular. This sense of interconnectedness holds them mindful of the influence of their decisions and actions on all species both now and in the distant future. These people acknowledge life on earth as a wonderful gift of the Creator with a sacred dimension to be cherished, indeed to be celebrated.

Flowing from this understanding is their absolute need to behave in a moral manner. From the study, it is easily discernible that these people operate from a profound moral commitment in their daily lives. It is clear that the ecological movement has motivated these actions in their lives. While endeavouring to live self-sufficiently, the core of their work involves caring for the environment and all the natural systems on earth in harmony with the great regulator – the Creator. There is a variety of ways of working to accomplish this, for example, production of organic food, use of natural composting and waste disposal systems, recycling methods, development of renewable resources, transport sharing and much more. Furthermore, as the findings point out, their prayer, reflection and meditation nourish the sacred character they experience in creation. The ecological movement has a major impact on spirituality today, renewing it within from without.

New Knowledge

Those in the ecological movement interviewed here all believe in God or in a higher power, which creates and sustains all things. Because of this they endeavour to behave in a particular manner, driven by that sense of the Divine acting benevolently in human affairs and indeed in all things. Their involvement in this movement has nourished their spirituality, enabling it to grow and develop.

However, I have observed that their beliefs and their search for meaning and the spirit of life has caused them to abandon to a large extent, the institution of religion. For example Christina has become very critical of organised religion, while Ruth declares 'that Churches and institutions manifesting power structures, defeat the very purpose they were established to serve.' Likewise Dorothy points out that inadequate spiritual nourishment from her adopted Church has urged her to search for something more. Indeed others have expressed similar sentiments.

The fact that a majority of deeply spiritual and baptised Christians, concretely living out their spirituality in the ecological movement, have consciously decided to leave the institutional Church is a challenge that emerges in the light of this work.

In the light of this, the Churches should take renewed cognisance of the values of the ecological movement in the world today and reflect its concerns direct pastoral activity towards its members. Otherwise genuine and deeply spiritual people will continue to drift away from the institution.

My findings suggest also that a majority of Christians involved in the ecological movement complain about a lack of spiritual nourishment within the institutional Church, a hunger they insist, that is satisfied for them in the ethos and lifestyle associated with this movement.

Flowing from this, greater attention needs to be given to the natural life cycles in liturgies and rituals.

Other suggestions include:

- holding special days to celebrate all life, the earth and its produce, ensuring participation of our youth
- becoming more involved at local level with caring for the earth, e.g. recycling programmes, environmental protection
- bringing groups together in relation to ecological issues ('Green Groups')
- offering surplus lands to groups involved in organic growing

In addition to one's intuitive sense of mystery nourished by religious faith, educational programmes, prayer and reflection can facilitate individuals in developing an increased awareness of the sacredness of creation – of the abundant material blessings flowing into each individual life from the earth itself. This in turn leads to active caring for the earth, for example, recycling, composting, organic growing, planting trees contributing to material transformation in many individual's lives. Finally, supporting the earth in producing its blessed abundance becomes part of the ritual of life acknowledging creation for what it is – a spiritual gift.

Notes

1 D. J. Hughes, *Ecology In Ancient Civilisations* (Albuquerque: University of New Mexico Press, 1975) 2-3, as quoted in R.A. Simkins, *Creator And Creation: Nature in the World View of Ancient Israel* (Massachusetts: Hendrickson, 1994), 3 n1.

2 M. Fox, *Creation Spirituality: Liberating Gifts for the Peoples of the Earth* (New York: Harper Collins, 1991) 7.

3 See T. Berry, *The Dream of the Earth* (San Francisco: Sierra Club, 1998) XI.

4 See H. Graham, *Soul Medicine: Restoring the Spirit to Healing* (Dublin: Gill & Macmillan Ltd, 2001)

5 S. McDonagh, *Why are We Deaf to the Cry of the Earth?* (Dublin: Veritas, 2001) 9.

6 S. Schneiders, 'Spirituality in the Academy', *Theological Studies* 50 (1989), 684 note 4.

7 E. Fromm, *Psychoanalysis and Religion* (New York, Vail-Ballou Press Inc. 1950 -1977) 21-30.

8 J. Wolski, Conn, 'Spirituality' in J. Kosmoschack et al., eds, *The New Dictionary of Theology* (Dublin: Gill & Macmillan, 1987).

9 D. Dorr, *Spirituality and Justice* (Dublin: Gill & Macmillan Ltd, 1984), 8-18.

10 H.P. Santmire, *Nature Reborn: The Theological and Cosmic Promise of Christian Theology* (Minneapolis: Augsburg Fortress, 2000), 100.

EPILOGUE

Dr Brian O'Leary SJ

Readers who have persevered this far in *Lamplighters: Exploring Spirituality in New Contexts* will have been exposed to absorbing presentations of the theory of 'action research' in the area of spirituality, as well as to examples of such research in the writings of some students at the Milltown Institute. The areas of research chosen by the latter represent aspects of our emerging self-confident, affluent, multi-cultural, but divided and spiritually ambivalent, society in Ireland at the beginning of the twenty-first century. The word 'postmodern' appears from time to time with all the implications of ambiguity, relativism, and rootlessness that it conveys. To explore such a society, its understanding of, attitude towards, and practice of spirituality, is bound to be worthwhile. The research will raise awareness in some readers, encourage deeper reflection in others, and may even point to a positive way forward into the future.

A few years ago an article of mine was published entitled 'Developments in Christian Spirituality since Vatican II'.[1] I have been looking again at its sub-headings to see how many of the topics that I had selected as significant were reflected in the students' essays. My sub-headings were: *Nostra Aetate* and inter-faith dialogue; The universal call to holiness; The Holocaust and Hiroshima; The journey inward; Religion and/or Spirituality?; The role of psychology; Freedom: inner – and outer; Church as *communio*; Spirituality at the margins; Women's experience; Ecological considerations. With the exception of 'The Holocaust and Hiroshima' (which may not have impinged sufficiently deeply on Irish consciousness) all of these topics form part of what the 'action research' discovered, surveyed and analysed. Some essays, of course, explored other phenomena such as the presence of immigrant communities among us, a trend that was still in the future in 1999. My brief reflections then on inter-faith dialogue were not rooted in the Irish experience. But now the increasingly multi-cultural, multi-faith dimension of the Irish scene is a challenge and a stimulus to a greater inclusiveness in society. The multi-layered spiritual values expressed by the term 'hospitality' apply to our relationships with immigrants as well as to our relationships with the marginalised and powerless in the indigenous community.

A disturbing theme running through some of the research is a disillusionment with the institutional Church, a sense of its inadequacy to meet the spiritual needs of ordinary people, especially those in problematic situations. There is the perception that the Church's teaching is somehow remote, if not irrelevant, and that in some areas of human experience the Church is silent when it should be speaking out. In a paradoxical way such views and judgements reveal the enormous expectations that people have of the Church. In some cases this may lead to the institutional Church becoming a scapegoat with all the sins and inadequacies of individuals and of society being laid at its door. But even when allowing for an element of this, it is a matter of serious concern that Christians of good intention and good will believe that they have to distance themselves from the institutional Church, and that some feel betrayed and hence partly or even totally alienated. In recent years much has been written about the causes of this development and there is no space to go over all the arguments and proposals for reform here. I would simply say that the word that came to me in this context was 'impoverishment'. The teaching of the institutional Church has (at least in Ireland) become impoverished because, in its determination to preserve doctrinal orthodoxy and moral rectitude, it has lost sight of the richness of its own spiritual tradition.

If this reads like a plug for the Milltown Institute's commitment to teaching and researching Christian spirituality (with an openness to other traditions), so be it! What it means to be a Christian can be described in many ways, beginning with a theology of baptism and Christian initiation. But being a Christian also includes a strong, existential, historical dimension, an awareness of standing within a tradition and being able to draw on the multiple resources that this tradition has garnered over the centuries. We have available to us the insights and wisdom of the Hebrew scriptures and the New Testament, of those who represent patristic and monastic theology and spirituality, of Patrick, Brigid and Colmcille, of Bernard and Hildegard, of Teresa and John of the Cross, of Ignatius and Mary Ward, of Thomas Merton and Dorothy Day. To be unaware of our history and tradition is to be unaware of who we are. Is this, at least in part, the reason why many people feel so rootless even within the Church? Is it because they do not know who their 'parents and grandparents' were in the family of the faith, the spiritual legacy that they have left us, the witness of how these women and men sought after and related with God? Not knowing the tradition of the ancestors means that in times of spiritual crisis many of to-day's Irish Christians are deprived of rich resources that could offer enlightenment, encouragement, hope and healing.

It was because of a consciousness of this pervasive deficit within Christian formation in Ireland that many people recently welcomed the collection of essays entitled *The Search for Spirituality: Seven Paths within the Catholic Tradition*.[2] Here was an accessible book, published in Ireland, that quarried a range of spiritualities and invited readers to enter into a living dialogue with them. In a different genre, or variety of genres, *Lamplighters: Spirituality in New Contexts* makes its own unique contribution to issues in spirituality, both experiential and theoretical. It breaks new ground in bringing the methodologies of 'action research', now well-established in other disciplines, to bear on the spiritualities that flourish (or are in decline) in Ireland today. There is much here to challenge the individual person in their self-awareness and spiritual growth, and even more to help the student or researcher to develop new tools and fresh ways of approaching the academic study of spirituality. *Lamplighters* merits a wide readership.

Notes

1   Brian O'Leary, 'Developments in Christian Spirituality since Vatican II', *Religious Life Review*, vol. 38, no. 197 (July-August 1999) 212-221, vol. 38, no.198 (September-October 1999) 314-315.

2   Stephen J. Costello (ed.), *The Search for Spirituality: Seven Paths within the Catholic Tradition*, (Dublin: Liffey Press, 2002).